"Look, Ja[...] someone, especially a stranger, watching your every move, and more so because you didn't ask for it, your boss did."

She paused to tamp down her frustration. "I've been where you are, back in the military, when I had to operate in combat situations that I hadn't been specifically trained for. As much as I was a fully trained Marine, my expertise isn't in the field as much as the office. I still needed the experts to help me get past some roadblocks, literally."

Do what a real CPA would do. Stay quiet.

"Is it fair to say you've never had any security training or personal protection before today?" Her voice softened and the gentle question grated. She wasn't intentionally patronizing, and if he were truly a novice in the world of security he'd probably appreciate her effort.

"Correct." His jaw tightened.

Dear Reader,

Welcome to the Pacific Northwest and the family-run security agency Cascade Confidential! If you've read my previous Harlequin Romantic Suspense miniseries, Silver Valley P.D., then you will recognize many of the same elements in this new one. Dedicated professionals working together to keep the world safe while facing down lethal villains, risking their very lives to do so. And did I mention they fall in love along the way?

In this first book of the miniseries, I loved putting together two agents who think the other is the criminal. Willow is a former Marine and recently began working for her family's very esteemed security agency. She's assigned to protect a man she at first sees as a numbers geek, but then assumes he's working on something far more sinister. Jay is an undercover FBI agent who assumes Willow is part of the crime syndicate he's intent on taking down. Imagine both their consternation when they find themselves intensely attracted to each other!

Besides romantic suspense, I write mystery novels. Keep up with my latest by subscribing to my newsletter via my website at gerikrotow.com. You can also follow me on Facebook at Facebook.com/gerikrotow and Instagram @geri_krotow.

Happy reading!

Peace,

Geri

AGENT UNDER WRAPS

GERI KROTOW

ROMANTIC SUSPENSE

Harlequin®
ROMANTIC SUSPENSE™

Recycling programs for this product may not exist in your area.

ISBN-13: 978-1-335-47161-1

Agent Under Wraps

Harlequin Enterprises ULC
22 Adelaide St. West, 41st Floor
Toronto, Ontario M5H 4E3, Canada
www.Harlequin.com

Printed in Lithuania

MIX
Paper | Supporting responsible forestry
FSC® C021394

Former naval intelligence officer and US Naval Academy graduate **Geri Krotow** draws inspiration from the global situations she's experienced. Geri loves to hear from her readers. You can email her via her website and blog, gerikrotow.com.

Books by Geri Krotow

Harlequin Romantic Suspense

Cascade Confidential

Agent Under Wraps

Silver Valley P.D.

Her Christmas Protector
Wedding Takedown
Her Secret Christmas Agent
Secret Agent Under Fire
The Fugitive's Secret Child
Reunion Under Fire
Snowbound with the Secret Agent
Incognito Ex
Stalked in Silver Valley

The Coltons of Grave Gulch

Colton Bullseye

The Coltons of Colorado

Stalking Colton's Family

Visit the Author Profile page
at Harlequin.com for more titles.

To Emily Sylvan Kim, agent and friend extraordinaire!
I wouldn't be having this much fun without
your unwavering support.

Chapter 1

"You do understand that I have never worked as a personal bodyguard, right?" Willow O'Malley spoke to her sister and boss, Toni, via her car's hands-free audio as she drove. The brand-new Ford Explorer, black with tinted windows for security, not status, was a company car. As she entered the highway westbound, toward the Washington state line and away from what had become her home base these last six months, her heart gave a little squeeze. It was validation that she had made a home of her rented condo with the view of Coeur d'Alene Lake, no matter that she was still new to a civilian lifestyle. "And while I'm at it, let me remind you that I'm not working for the family biz to be a glorified babysitter."

"You've mentioned your concerns at least six times since last night, yes." Toni's indulgent tone said it all. She really did need Wil to handle this last-minute contract request. The family private security agency, Cascade Confidential, kept its physical headquarters in Seattle, Washington, where their mother had founded it decades earlier. Although they were used to steady growth, this past year had seen almost exponential increase in requests and clients. There were plenty of people applying for their many open positions, but security clearances took time, sometimes months.

Because CC took government contracts, their employees not only had to have US government clearances but also had to pass the tight vetting that CC adhered to.

"How much is this contract worth, by the way?" Wil asked.

Toni told her, and Wil shook her head. "Holy cow, sis. That's enough to pay for Sierra's entire college education." Wil still wasn't used to the significant increase in salary that her military skills commanded in the "real" world, as her fellow Marines had called life after the Corps.

"It is, indeed, but don't forget we recently bought three SUVs, the same model as yours, and there's always the astronomical company overhead."

Any discussion of financials made Wil's eyes roll, no matter that she comprehended that the top security services provided by CC cost top dollar. She respected the job her sister did as CEO, no question. But when it came to numbers, unless it had to do with the website location of a cyberterrorist or the details of the cold case she was working on, it didn't interest her.

"Point taken. We need this job. And I don't mean to yank your chain so much, but I'm the only one in the Coeur d'Alene office who's been working the Hartford girls cold case, not to mention the cyberhacking cases I briefed you on last week." Wil had thought she'd be spending most of her time solving cybercrime for their clients, but last week an elderly woman had come into the office and showed proof that she was the grandmother of an eleven-year-old girl who had disappeared, along with two other girls, thirty years ago. She was determined to find answers for the woman.

"It's all going to wait until I get back from this godforsaken assignment." Wil needed to be fully immersed in a case to connect all the loose threads that were inevitably there. This bodyguard assignment was more than a distraction; it was a threat to her solving her first big cold case for Cascade Confidential. It was also her first civilian case that didn't involve cyber ops, a chance to prove her mettle in a different situation.

"You don't have to remind me that you're the computer and cold case genius, Wil. It's part of the reason I asked you to leave the Marine Corps earlier than you'd planned." The bigger reason was left unspoken: The family-run security agency was stretched to breaking with a tsunami of requests and limited personnel to assign. The deeper, private reason she'd agreed to come work for Toni, however, was that she needed something different, a life change that involved more than another new duty station assignment. She'd never intended to make the Corps a career. Not at first, anyway.

But one day had bled into the next, and her tours of duty piled up to a dozen moves over the last twenty years, not including the several deployments downrange, often to remote duty stations, including one combat tour. If asked, she wouldn't be able to articulate any one reason she'd decided to leave the Corps, which she was forever bonded to. It was something deep inside her that had urged the change.

Her most recent Marine Corps assignment had been the Pentagon, where her life—and practically her soul—weren't her own. The break from 24-7 cybersecurity responsibilities was an unexpected bonus of working for her family. The yoke of global security, even though it had been shared with her colleagues from all the other military branches around the globe, had been soul crushing. Now, she was energized when she awoke each morning. The freedom of working her own hours, whether at home with her spectacular lake view, or in the tastefully appointed Coeur d'Alene office, was exhilarating.

Another factor that nudged her to make the switch to a civilian lifestyle was that Wil had discovered she had a talent for cold cases. The military cyber cold case had been a onc-off, though, at least for a Marine. She'd not likely have another cold case while on active duty.

When the local Hartford girls cold case had fallen into her lap, it validated her decision to leave the Corps and come home to the Pacific Northwest, PNW.

"As much as I want you to solve hacking and cold cases for us, we need all hands working the agency's front line right now. Face it—you're the only one of us with personal security training, thanks to your time in the Corps. You know that, sis." Toni O'Malley's chiding tone reminded Wil of when they were kids and Toni convinced her that she was the only one who could climb onto the counter—Wil had always been more athletically inclined than Toni—to steal cookies from the jar for all of them. Which usually meant she was setting up Wil to take the heat while placating their younger siblings with the sugary treats. "Like I said, I hope to have someone to relieve you before the end of the weekend, by Monday at the latest. We're strapped on manpower until the Seattle aerospace conference is over. Honestly, Wil? I don't know if I'm coming or going these days. Late summer's turned into early autumn and our workload shows no signs of letting up," Toni said.

"You're an expert at juggling, Toni. Look at what a good mother you are, and how much you do for the community, too." She left out the part about her elder sis running CC, a multimillion-dollar business with over two hundred permanent employees and thousands who were on a contract basis.

"Thanks, Wil. I'm so relieved you came home. I'm lucky you're my sister. You're my lifeline."

"So you tell me." Wil considered herself the lucky one. For twenty years, she'd served in the United States Marine Corps, both Stateside and abroad. While in uniform her only concern had been her mission and completing it. Politics, local events like an aerospace industry conference simply hadn't been a concern. But now, every large-scale gathering of people in the Pacific Northwest, from rock concerts to sporting events to political campaign rallies, could affect Wil's workload.

Every public event was fraught with security concerns. Local law enforcement, be it police, sheriffs or state troopers, couldn't keep up with it all. Nor should they, in Wil's opinion. Law enforcement had enough on its shoulders than to act as crowd control. There simply weren't enough bodies in uniform to handle it all. Hence private security firms like her family's were inundated with requests for large-event security year-round. It meant a boon for their firm's coffers, but also was a drain on her and her four siblings as their firm had expanded.

"You're the only one I can trust with this on such short notice, Wil." Toni must have interpreted Wil's silence as disagreement. She never doubted her sister was still on the line, as they had always enjoyed a close relationship and were comfortable with long periods of silence in their conversations.

"You're the boss." Wil spoke as she maneuvered through an S curve. And she meant it. It had been bittersweet to leave the Corps and the many troops she'd led. But it was nice to not have to make the big decisions, too. While all of their siblings got together via a monthly conference call to handle CC strategic initiatives, Toni was their CEO for day-to-day operations.

"I'm not feeling very in charge lately, but you know how it goes."

"I do. Hey, Toni?" Wil accelerated past a slow-moving tractor trailer hauling a full load of logs, recently harvested, as the damp, rough bark illuminated by her headlights looked fresh. A whiff of fresh cedar aroma reached through her air vent. She'd missed this distinct scent of her child-hood for too long on too many overseas assignments. Any job in the Pacific Northwest at any time of day, even at o-dark-thirty, like now, was better than being away from her home and family roots.

"Yeah?"

"You know I'm on your side, right? You're the best boss, no matter how chaotic it feels to you right now. We'll push past this." Wil meant it. She had missed their sisterly ban-ter that only frequent communication nurtured. Being sta-tioned on the other side of the globe had prevented her and her siblings from the welcome repartee. "Please don't mis-take my reluctance about this case for unwillingness. I don't want to disappoint you, is all. Marine Corps basic training, combined with the short class you sent me to last month, is the sum total of my bodyguard experience." Which in her opinion meant zilch. Nada.

"Got it. I know I can count on you, sis." Toni's relief doused some of the frazzled nerves Wil detected in her sis-ter's normally honey-smooth voice. "It's been insane since Mom and Dad retired." The timing of which had propelled Willow's "someday" about working for the family business to turn into "right now."

"Yeah, the nerve of them wanting to enjoy their golden years." They both had a good laugh at the expense of the parents they adored but whose help they could really use right now. "How dare they leave us all with a booming business and escape to their forever home in Montana." Wil's stomach dropped. "Oh no! Their party is less than a month away. I need to put it in my phone. I keep forgetting." She'd been so deep in launching the Idaho satellite office and working on her pet project that she'd lost track of time. Again. Their parents were hosting a housewarming of the gargantuan "cabin" they'd built at the base of the mountains outside Bozeman. "But seriously, do you think they know what we're up to, with the surprise party?"

Toni snorted. "Are you kidding? Mom's too busy putting the last touches on the house, and Dad's been spending all of his time doing whatever Mom tells him to." She chuckled. "They'll be surprised, all right."

"I can't imagine being with anyone for fifty years. Not to mention having five kids over a span of fourteen years like Mom did." Wil's words were certain, but her breath hitched as her heart beat in silent regret. It wasn't that she never wanted a family, but that she'd been too busy to ever seriously consider it, save for one brief time when she'd been dating someone she'd thought was the perfect man. "Not that I could be married for five decades, at this point. I mean, Mom and Dad met so young."

"You're only thirty-eight! Give me a break. You never know what's just around the corner." Toni's positivity had to be overcompensation for both of their sad love lives.

"Statistics are pretty consistent, Toni. It's going to be you, Aubrey, and me all the way until we're nonagenarians, sis. Let our brothers worry about carrying on the family name. We'll be the aunts who spoil their kids." Wil was the middle of the siblings, with two older sisters Toni and Aubrey—the VP of operations—both working in Seattle, and their two younger brothers Kevin and Jake handling forensics and surveillance, respectively. There was seven years between Wil and their oldest brother, Kevin.

"Whatever." Toni's crisp professional tone was back, shutting down the topic. "I've got to go. Text me when you're on-site and keep us apprised of your status, as always."

"Copy."

Toni disconnected, and Wil switched the car audio to her favorite playlist. Hard rock, loud and fast. It was her go-to in the gym when she'd had to stay in shape through combat tours and still a great motivational set of blood-pumping music. She belted out the lyrics to a crankin' Guns N' Roses oldie, thankful no one else could hear her. She figured it was her last chance to not be bored out of her mind for the next seventy-two hours. Sure, Toni had promised another security agent would relieve her by Monday, but Wil knew better than to count on it. If Toni had to tap her for the glorified babysitting contract, odds were there wasn't another decent prospect for the job, even after the aerospace conference ended. CC had a long pipeline for new hires, which included months of background checks, rigorous training both physically and in classroom settings, and a final certification exam that involved a week at their remote safe house location. It was why CC had the reputation it did and could command the fees that gave even their most wealthy clients pause. But as their motto said, foolproof security was priceless.

It might very well be her only assignment for a week or so.

She snorted as she took the exit onto a winding mountain road and turned the music down to a dull roar. At least this contract would be a break from the insane pace she'd been keeping since returning home and joining CC full-time. She knew she was a high-energy person and thrived on working several cases at once. But setting up the Coeur d'Alene office, along with digging into the decades-old cold case, had left her pretty well spent. She couldn't help it; once she was down the gopher trail of research—of a cold case or cyberattack—only a direct order from her superior to cease could pull her out.

Toni's encouragement to "remember, your first priority is to get the Idaho office going and to bring in new customers in the area" had shown her there was a hell of a lot more criminal activity in western Washington and Idaho than she'd ever expected, much of it going back to the last century.

Wil's mind began to race with all the possibilities for the cold case that involved the disappearance of three young girls in the early 1990s. While she knew the chances were slim that the kidnapped girls would still be alive, at the very least she wanted answers for the families who suffered from the loss to this day.

The girls' last location had been in western Washington, falling under the Coeur d'Alene office's territory. Since then, Wil had done some digging of her own to familiarize herself with the historical facts. Coincidentally, the girls had disappeared within a few miles of the logging company's headquarters, where Wil was headed. No matter, as right now it had to take a back seat to keeping a corporate employee safe.

"You're my lifeline, Wil."

Recalling Toni's words, she refocused on the pertinent details of this spur-of-the-moment job.

Apparently a logging—or was it manufacturing, maybe both?—company outside Spokane had been the target of some recent threats, all of which the business's private security had so far handled. Except over the last several days, there had been not one but three death threats aimed at the most significant members of the staff. Wil couldn't help suppressing a grin as she remembered Toni telling her that her particular person to protect was the company's accountant. Not the sexiest position, in her opinion.

A number cruncher.

In the Marine Corps and Navy—its sister service—finances fell under the Navy's supply branch, unceasingly teased for its cushy living conditions compared to Marines assigned to operational units. Yes, every Marine was a combat soldier, but there was perceived status among various military operational specialties.

She shook her head, thinking of the raucous laughter retelling this assignment to her former colleagues would elicit. How, after years of stalking and breaking the backs of the most challenging and subversive foreign military hackers, Wil was now getting paid almost three times as much…to protect a numbers geek.

The circuitous route to the company's headquarters turned steep, and she engaged the SUV's four-wheel drive. GPS showed another half mile to her destination. There was nothing out here except rough road and trees. Lots and lots of trees.

Yeah, the next few days were going to be very, very quiet in comparison to her usual pace.

Chapter 2

*A*lmost there.

The sun was shooting streaks of pale light through the trees that lined the road, and Wil adjusted her rearview mirror to keep the glare from obscuring her vision. The highway had yielded to a two-lane route through what seemed to be a flatter area, but she knew she was heading back into the thick of the mountains. Mack Logging & Manufacturing was smack dab in the middle of the foothills of the Selkirk mountains, which extended east and north into Idaho and Canada. This meant that the small town she spied just ahead was probably going to be it for any civilization between here and there. There had been a single woebegone gas station upon exiting the highway, but she'd seen a sign for fresh-brewed coffee, "only one mile away," and her inner coffee monster stirred. One great thing about Washington, and the PNW in general, was the myriad independent coffee roasters and brewers.

Welcome to Pine Hills

The sign appeared no more than a quarter of a mile before the town rose up as if out of nowhere, with charming Victorian homes and businesses sprinkling either side of the road. She figured the coffee shop had to be where all the cars were parked at an angle, nose-in, or at least close to it.

It was still an hour before Mack's office hours, enough time to grab a cuppa and read over the sparse PDF document that summarized the contract between CC and Mack. Toni had emailed it in the wee hours of the morning, while Wil was still asleep, dreaming of going into her office this morning and working cases she was intimately familiar with.

This assignment was definitely unknown territory for her.

She shut off the engine and grabbed her small wallet out of her cranberry-red leather bag and departed her vehicle. Instead of the aroma of coffee, however, the distinct aroma of bacon punctuated with flour and sugar wafted out of the door that had just opened, its attached bell tinkling a welcome. She looked at the words painted on the large window. Not a coffee shop, a restaurant. Waffle and Egg Diner.

"Going in?" A gray-bearded man in a flannel shirt and suspenders kept the door open with a meaty hand.

"I—" She opened her mouth to refuse at the same time her stomach growled. She looked at her phone to verify the time, then grinned. "Why not?"

"You can't come to Pine Hills and not stop at Joe's. And you won't go wrong with the waffles." His parting shot was welcome but unnecessary. Once inside, she bypassed the hostess and took the single empty stool at the low, retro Formica counter. Seated between two men, she didn't care to make small talk and was grateful when neither of them did, either.

Wil cherished her alone time, and this might be her last solo meal for the next few days, if not more, depending on the living situation her client had and whether or not she could eat separately while also keeping an eye on him.

The coffee wasn't coffee-shop grade, but it was still excellent, and her meal even more so. She'd forgone the waffle when she'd spotted eggs Benedict, her favorite, on the chalkboard menu that hung above the refrigerated shelves replete with pies and puddings.

"Use the company credit card for all expenses."

Toni had been clear that it was far easier for both Wil as well as their accounting office to keep track of her expenditures, and reimburse her more promptly, if she used the card. But Wil had no time to spare after she gulped down her third cup of coffee, and eyeing the long line at the cashier, she opted to pay in cash. She pulled out a twenty and placed it atop the paper bill the waitress had left.

And inadvertently hit the hand of the man next to her, who was doing the exact same thing.

"Excuse me." She pulled her hand back and went to stand. Just as the man stood. They bumped shoulders, or rather, her shoulder bumped into his upper arm. The dude had to be almost a foot taller than her five feet five inches. She'd made an erroneous assumption that everyone here was a logger, forester or similar. She recognized her error when she realized the man whose chest she was unexpectedly eye level with sported running gear.

Wil's gaze followed the three-quarter zip tech fabric top to where it opened and revealed the collar of a dark green shirt, and further up, the scruffy throat and chin— ignoring how the definitive Adam's apple and cleft made her hormones take notice—and looked up at the person she'd ignored for the last thirty minutes. She tried to offer a quick smile.

"I—" Her mouth froze, open in surprise as she stared into the most intense blue eyes she'd ever seen. Apparently this man had thought, like her, he'd been sitting next to just another nondescript diner. Because as she continued to maintain eye contact with him, a flash of awareness sparked in his irises, and she caught a slight twitch to his incredibly sensuous lips.

Wow.

Too bad she hadn't noticed her fellow diner sooner. But why would she have? He wore a dark knit cap pulled low over his brow, and his nondescript athletic jacket covered what appeared to be broad shoulders and flat abs.

"Pardon me." He wasn't looking at her as he pulled bills out of a worn leather wallet.

"No frets." *No frets?* Gah. She sounded like an idiot.

Since he showed absolutely zero interest in conversing further, she focused on paying her own bill. Had she imagined his interest only seconds ago? When he turned and left the diner, she couldn't help but check out the rest of him. As she surreptitiously took in his legs, dressed in slim-fitting joggers, Wil smiled at his high-end running shoes, the same brand as hers. She recognized them because she was a runner, too.

He exited the diner but not before she caught a solid glance of his butt. The stranger boasted the nicely sculpted ass many runners had. The mystery man didn't bother to look at her again, the bell over the door tinkling its happy notes as it shut behind him.

Desire curled tight in her belly as heat flooded her cheeks. Why did a complete stranger who showed absolutely no interest in her get her sexy going? *Double gah.*

Maybe she needed to give her lack of a dating life a closer look after this weekend.

Wil beat her own path to the exit, grateful that she didn't have to stop at the cash register and talk to anyone. She knew from experience that her blushing made her pale skin look like she'd either spent a day outside without sun protection or was incredibly flustered. She was embarrassed at her momentary lack of composure, sure, but what bothered her more was that she'd completely forgotten why she was in a diner in the middle of bum freak nowhere to begin with.

Remember your mission. She was here for a job. A contract, and one that didn't include looking for or finding love along the way. She forced errant thoughts of the sexy runner from her mind as she walked to her car.

Unlocking the vehicle's door, she paused, hand still on the handle. Her nape prickled under her dark ball cap, and it wasn't from her tight ponytail. She wished the sensation was unfamiliar and didn't throw her mind back to her brief exposure to combat.

But the feeling she was being watched shot tingles down her neck, across her shoulders, into her gut, tightening it into a knot. Wil pretended her shoelace was untied and bent over, covertly scanning the area in her immediate vicinity. The diner was set in a clearing that included a concrete slab for the log building and a graveled parking area in front and around two of its sides. Everywhere else, all she could see was line after line of cedar and pine trees. She was technically located on the main road that ran through town, but as she straightened she was painfully aware of the isolation the trees provided, how remote this tiny town was. Cozy if one·wanted to have a meal or a cuppa on the covered portico, but deadly if you were being stalked. In the enemy's sights.

Dried fern fronds waved in the slight, cooler breeze, as if saying goodbye to summer as fall set in. The crackling sound made by the movement drew her attention to a shadow, a tall shadow, at the edge of her line of sight. Before she could discern if it was two- or four-legged, she found herself staring at the backside of her silent breakfast companion as he ran off in the opposite direction.

Her breath hitched, her hands fisted. Pure reflex screamed at her to run after the man, shake him down, figure out what he was doing so close to her parking spot.

Calm down. He's not an enemy, not an assailant.

Even if he was, he wasn't her problem. Doing the job Toni and CC asked of her was all she needed to worry about. She let out a long sigh. Mystery man was going for a run, good for him. Running right after eating had never been her forte, but to each his own.

Forcing herself to refocus, Wil fully opened the door and climbed up onto the plush leather driver's seat and ignited the hybrid engine with the press of a button. She grinned. The reminder that she was back in the States, in her native city's backyard, yanked her out of her anxiety. Did she ever think she'd be driving a hybrid model of what had forever been a gas-guzzler? Would she have ever trusted anything but a one hundred percent gas powered V-8 engine, or better, a Marine utility combat vehicle?

Welcome to the real world. "Real" was the adjective heard most often while on active duty and making reference to life outside of the Marine Corps. Away from all she'd known since she'd been a bright-eyed eighteen-year-old recruit. Away from the several men she'd dated, and the one who'd broken her heart. For good.

She sighed and took a sip of the coffee she'd taken, to go. It was still two hours before her showtime at the logging company, and while she planned to show up early, more than fifteen minutes ahead of time was too much.

She'd sit here a while, go over the contract, and if she had time left she'd review the notes she made yesterday about the cold case, to keep the facts alive for at least her subconscious while she fulfilled this personal protection contract. Because she'd left the house so early, she'd left the finishing touches on her appearance for now. She tossed her ballcap into the passenger seat, applied her minimalist makeup, and let her hair down. First impressions lasted and she wanted to appear as a polished professional.

With each sip of coffee, those blue eyes flashed in her mind's eye. Her heart would never be ready for love again, but that didn't mean she wasn't uninterested in dating. Just not yet.

And definitely not with some random blue-eyed dude.

Chapter 3

Jay swore to himself as he picked up his pace, pushed to increase the distance between him and the diner parking lot as fast as his thirty-five-year-old legs would allow.

Making prolonged eye contact with the beauty in the diner was too close for Jay's comfort. He'd never noticed her before. And he would have. Her smart business-casual attire, complete with those stretchy, formfitting business slacks that shaped more like yoga or running tights, had left little to his imagination. Her bright hazel eyes contrasted with hair a shade of vivid copper speckled with rust, the same color as the underbelly of his much beloved beat-up pickup. Most of the folks he regularly saw at early breakfast were locals, including the women. Hardworking in the logging industry, for the most part. The red-haired beauty must be some kind of professional along the lines of attorney, insurance agent or similar. He'd lingered behind the large overgrowth at the forest's edge until he confirmed that she'd gotten into a vehicle, noting its make, model and license tag. Just in case.

She was a complete stranger, in all probability he'd never see her again, but it didn't matter. Jay trusted no one.

And no one should trust you. Not now, maybe not ever. He still hadn't decided if he'd stay in this line of work after this particular assignment. He laughed, and it took him a second to realize he'd done so aloud, unfettered. He looked around. There was no one in the immediate vicinity.

Phew.

He swore again. Was he going to let one hot woman shake his resolve, distract him from what he'd dreamed of for years?

He'd enjoyed running to the diner for breakfast most days since starting this new job, which in truth was his last stop in a long line of steps to get here. To the best, most dangerous job of his life.

Running the perimeter of his property before taking the half mile wooded path into town had become his favorite part of the day. Fun, even. Before he had to report to the job that, while he was aware of its importance, he'd never describe as fun.

He was used to keeping to himself, blending in, appearing like any other corporate refugee who'd traded in their surefire white-collar job to work from home as a private contractor in the depths of the PNW, or as a temporary employee at one of the few offices in the area.

Plus, the diner's maple bacon–ham omelet beat microwaved oatmeal any day.

"Hey, Jones, buddy, you have those stats from the Logan deal ready yet? Boss is breathing down my neck for them."

"Give me a few." Jay nodded at the man standing on the other side of his cubicle wall as if he really cared about his immediate supervisor's stress levels, or the numbers on his open spreadsheet. He was here to bring down the arm-candy-wife-turned-CEO and the crime syndicate she'd taken over from her now ailing elderly husband. Veronica Clayton orchestrated her evil empire from the comfort of her office during work hours and from her family's multimillion-dollar estate after quitting time.

He still wasn't used to being referred to by his last name, probably because it was an alias. Jayden Lambert, FBI special agent, was Jay Jones, CPA to everyone at Mack Logging & Manufacturing headquarters.

This was the assignment of his lifetime, the case he'd spent years prepping for. He'd gone so far as to learn more advanced accounting skills in order to be able to get inserted into the company on short notice when his informant in an unwitting sister syndicate back east recommended him to Mack CEO Veronica Clayton. He wasn't a CPA, as his fake résumé touted, but so far no one had questioned his work, a fact known to him thanks to the steadfast feedback he received from his team at headquarters in Washington, DC. They hadn't really given much weight to his résumé, either, he assumed. His procurement of this position had been all due to word of mouth, and even money passing hands in face-to-face meetings, surprisingly common in this digital age.

The world might be all about cyber, but Jay's job still relied on face-to-face and old-fashioned long hours of analysis and law-abiding operations. He'd been told by Derek to "keep it all smooth" upon his arrival, which was Mack Logging & Manufacturing for "make sure we don't get audited." It was a fair enough directive from a law-abiding company. But after only two days, he'd quickly validated what he already knew from months—years—of intelligence gathering. Mack was in a dirty business, stained with innocent blood.

Mack Logging & Manufacturing, along with its associated industries, were for the most part legit, legal. But a slight scratch below the surface of the financial figures reflected that Mack had been a front company for money laundering for decades, totally under the government's radar. All because the first line of government bureaucracy included local tax collectors and small-town accountants who had accepted bribes to cook the books more than the smoked salmon that was a winter staple in the PNW.

Some time in the last year, however, the faux figures began hiding much more sinister actions, and ominous hints of what was to come for the syndicate.

"A few secs is all you have, my man." Derek's faux-collegial tone grated, and not just because he'd interrupted Jay's deep thoughts. Derek was the epitome of a grating, ass-kissing personality.

"On it." Jay clenched his jaw to keep from even thinking about how he'd like to let Derek know he wasn't his *buddy* or *man* but instead the guy who was going to put Derek behind bars for most of his consequential life. If he did his job right and didn't mess up the takedown, that is.

Derek Michaels was close in age to Jay, but that's where their similarities ended. The CFO—in name only; the man had zero numbers skills—and apparent right-hand lackey to the CEO had no sense of personal space or professional boundaries. He expected Jay to not only provide detailed reports on short notice, but to join him at the spanking-new recreational facility located a short walk across Mack headquarters' graveled lot. Not to lift weights, box or play racquetball. No, Derek liked to play pickleball, which to Jay was little more than big-boy Ping-Pong. But he had to admit, the name of the game was ironic. The company was in a pickle with law enforcement they'd yet to figure out.

Based on what he'd garnered by listening to employees grouse in the sparsely appointed break room, the gym, pool and spa had been installed earlier this year after Veronica took full control of Mack's reins. It definitely had not been built at the behest of ninety-two-year-old Cal Clayton, the founder of Mack, who lay in a coma at their estate, reportedly near death for at least the last six months. That was what his FBI intelligence reports revealed, and a press release by Mack that announced Veronica's assumption of CEO duties so that "Clayton can focus on his legacy." The large, glossy plaque in the front foyer boasted a smiling Cal Clayton and glowing description of how he'd started the company with his bare hands and saw it become a Fortune 500 LLC over several decades. The last line read, "...Clayton's legacy of hard work and providing for Pacific Northwest families is sure to continue." Since he'd been working here, though, he'd barely heard the old man's name mentioned. *Some legacy.*

Jay stared at the computer screen and let his fingers fly, ignoring Derek's coffee breath and, worse, his overbearing demeanor. Derek's phone dinged, another annoyance. Jay was used to leaving his phone "at the door" whenever he worked either at FBI offices or undercover. No one at Mack seemed to understand the value of putting their phones on silent, or at least vibrate, mode.

You'd have your ringer up loud, too, if Veronica was your boss.

While he believed that most of the two hundred employees at Mack headquarters had no clue that the company was, in fact, a money-laundering front for the Pacific Northwest's largest trafficking syndicate—drugs and rumored humans—Veronica Clayton's ruthlessness was renowned and respected. Screw up? Expect to be on the street. No second chances. Veronica's idea of a second chance was a slit throat. That had been the coroner's determination of cause of death for the most recent body, discovered near a local landfill, just moments before it would have been buried for all eternity. The local law enforcement types who'd been put on this case had done a bang-up job to date, and Jay couldn't wait for the day he could thank them personally.

But he'd never met them. For now, Jay was a geeky accountant doing the bidding of Cal Clayton's arm candy spouse–turned–CEO.

"Forget the report, Jay-man. We gotta go. Boss says time's up. Now." Derek slapped the fabric-covered wall, causing the charts Derek had thumbtacked to it to tremble.

"One sec. I'll have it—"

"No, Jones. Did you hear what I said? *Now.*" Derek looked down at him with eyes that had begun to bulge ever so slightly. He reminded Jay of a turkey vulture—no predatory skills of his own but totally dependent on a raptor's kill.

CEO Veronica Clayton was every bit a raptor. And she wanted to see him, in person, right now. With or without the spreadsheets.

"Come on!" Derek's voice trembled more than growled, and the sliver of trepidation he'd kept at bay, had to tamp down in order to maintain his undercover persona, oozed out of its hiding place in his consciousness.

Jay didn't reply, nor did he have time to dwell on his observations as he stood, hiked up his too-large trousers—he purposely dressed in cheap, oversized clothing to appear nerdy and sorely missed the well-fitting suits he wore as an agent—and fell into step behind Derek. His supervisor never allowed him to walk alongside him. Another tell as far as Jay was concerned. He'd learned to read body language with the best of them, and a tell was an action or gesture that unwittingly betrayed a person's emotions.

Derek was a man with big insecurities that were rooted

deep down in the rat hole of his soul. But his anxiety wasn't unwarranted, and the coil of tension that had lived in Jay's gut since he'd finally arrived at this last stage of his investigation threatened to blossom into flat-out fear. Even FBI agents had their moments of urgent caution, he reminded himself. But it didn't stop his knees from threatening to turn to blobs of gelatin. Had the CEO found out Jay's true identity? Her syndicate had myriad moles, in and out of the government, and while still undercover back East he'd identified a syndicate mole whom he thought he'd fooled. That man had given Jay's undercover persona the gravitas it required to enter Veronica's inner circle. Had he been found out?

Was this it, then? All his hours, sweat, countless career risks? Had it come down to taking a bullet—he didn't let his mind go to the other more grisly possibilities—before he'd had time to blow open the criminal syndicate Veronica Clayton had married into and now ran with her manicured fist?

Jay and Derek entered the CEO suite and were immediately waved past by Mack Logging & Manufacturing's reception, which consisted of a burly bald man in a fleece vest that sported the company logo: ML&M embroidered in red across a tall pine tree. The image was innocuous enough, until one peered closer and saw the wolf, fangs visible, peering out from behind the branches. Impressive what graphic arts were capable of these days. Surprising that there weren't a few threads of scarlet dripping down from the wolf's jaw. Was Jay's blood soon to be shed?

At least I'll take my sense of humor to the grave. But he'd really like to bring down this entire diabolical syndicate with him.

They stepped into the CEO's inner sanctum, and not for

the first time Jay wondered at how much of it had been re-furbished for its most recent occupant. The expansive space of cream wainscoting with sage-green walls might exude professionalism, but it belied the masculine power that had created and grown not only a lethal crime syndicate but a remarkable cover business that still operated some legit logging and respectable manufacturing. He'd overheard an employee remark that Veronica had had the entire of-fice suite redone two weeks after her husband had taken ill. Certainly not the move of a shocked, caring spouse, he thought. His own father had been his now-deceased mother's caretaker through the rough road the entire fam-ily had traveled with her early-onset Alzheimer's. And he knew his mother would have done the same for Dad, if need be. Veronica Clayton's manner of handling her in-valid husband synced with the intelligence gleaned from her house staff—that rumors about exactly how the elder Clayton had become bedridden abounded.

"Gentlemen." Veronica Clayton's cool voice cut through his thoughts. Today's outfit was the usual for her—busi-ness on top with lethal sexy on the bottom. She wore a silk blouse, tailored suit jacket, heavy makeup made to look natural, long brunette hair cut in a striking style that em-phasized her steely beauty and sharp dark eyes. But that was only part of her getup, the warm-up. What had prob-ably landed Veronica in Cal Clayton's orbit to begin with was displayed on full view in the bottom half of her ap-pearance. Her miniskirt—also tailored, he guessed, by how perfectly it matched her jacket and hugged every curve she possessed—revealed long legs encased in sheer black stock-ings, further elongated by her sky-high heels. A typical desk would only reveal the top half of Veronica's outfit, but this CEO sat at a massive, completely clear, glass-topped desk. Veronica Clayton employed whatever means necessary to achieve her goals, and sexual distraction wasn't beneath her.

"Sorry for the delay, boss. My man Jay here is still adjusting to our operational pace." Derek flashed his crapeating grin, but it didn't hide his simpering. He pointed to the seats arrayed in front of her desk and elbowed Jay. "C'mon—"

"Don't take a seat. This isn't going to take long." Veronica emphasized her command with a hand held up in the universal gesture for *stop*. Jay remained in place, as he hadn't sat, but Derek wobbled on his feet, his air of superiority momentarily knocked from his obnoxious bravado. In any other setting, Jay would enjoy his own version of a crap-eating grin. Except he had to focus on keeping his own legs steady, to push back the primal, natural fear he'd felt before. When facing down a drug kingpin or, in his last undercover role, a corrupt agent.

No matter. He played his role to the best of his ability, keeping his expression bland, unknowing. Could anyone else hear his heartbeat?

Veronica's gaze narrowed, sparks of frustration in her eyes. He prayed her angst was with Derek and not him, forced himself to keep breathing, to ignore the warning sensations gnawing at his insides.

"As you both are aware, we've had several threats against Mack recently. Our security team has identified some of the perpetrators. We have the usual half dozen or so pesky environmentalists, which isn't what I'm worried about. What's caught my attention is that we've received at least one threat toward our financial systems in the form of a cyberattack, and we've had threats that indicate our personnel are being targeted. We're fairly certain that several if not all are from one of our favorite disenfranchised former employees, but there could be others who are still upset at being let go last month. Honestly, you'd think no one had ever been fired before." She shook her head in mock exasperation.

"No matter how weak each individual threat is, however, I can't discount the possibility that bad luck could strike and we'd be hit with several threats at once. We happen to be in the middle of several negotiations surrounding mergers with other companies. Threats could come from any of those businesses, who perceive my motives as somewhat unscrupulous, which of course is ridiculous."

Did she really think she was convincing anyone who knew who she truly was with this baloney soliloquy?

"Our security is top-notch, of course, but it's come to my attention that we could use a few more helping hands with our employees' security. I don't want any member of my elite security team to be burdened with routine guarding and protection, not right now. And as you know, I take my employees' safety very seriously." Veronica's small smile was smug. Jay was never surprised by the self-importance of crime bosses, but he had to admit, albeit only to himself, that Veronica Clayton took the meaning of *ruthless* to a new level.

"Usually we'd have in-house security step up to personal protection, but our resources are a bit…" A blindingly white tooth caught the inside of her lower lip. A tiny, almost invisible movement, but Jay was a master at observation. It was what made him such a good undercover agent. "We're expanding business at such a quick rate, every single employee is stretched thin. Since I won't tolerate anything less than one hundred percent assurance when it comes to our security, I've hired out a private contractor for our top financial resource." She gave Jay a quick nod. "Your talents haven't gone unnoticed."

Wait, the personal security was for *him*?

The best-laid undercover plans are tentative at best. Words of wisdom he'd laughed at with his class in the FBI Academy.

"...temporarily. This will all be history before you know it," Veronica had continued, oblivious to Jay's shock. *Phew.* But what was she talking about, when she said it would all be "history" soon? The end, or beginning, of the enormous crime syndicate merger he suspected was about to go down? Or were the cartels and local syndicates rivals? Was he looking at a bloodbath?

Was Veronica planning a turf war? Turf being mostly digital these days, but it would involve loss of life. Veronica never hesitated to eliminate anyone who got in her way, and if she had her sights on a syndicate takeover, the current bosses wouldn't go out unless they were dead. It's how it played out through centuries of gangs, rings, syndicates, cartels. Loyalty until death.

"Boss, do you really think that's such a good idea? Bringing in an outsider just for an accountant? For this guy? I carry a gun, you know." Derek's tone was at once patronizing and earnest. And his assessment was so far off the mark. *Good. You're doing your job.* "Jay is never out of my sight when he's here."

No kidding. Since his arrival a little over a month ago, Derek had stayed glued to Jay. The last thing Jay needed was a second babysitter. He knew this was all part of Mack protocol when it came to the more sensitive parts of the business. There was nothing of higher stakes to a money-laundering operation than its financial records. Jay hadn't been asked to cook the books yet, but it was merely a matter of time.

"You're not a bodyguard, Derek," Veronica snapped.

"Why would anyone be upset with me?" Jay fought to use words a civilian would and not ask why a former employee would target him.

"That's not your concern." Veronica stood and gazed past Jay's shoulder. "But Wil O'Malley is. Come on in, Wil."

The soft swish of fabric on fabric reached his ears as a fourth person entered the room. Footfalls didn't sound in Veronica's office due to the thickly piled carpet, which he suspected was to support Veronica's stiletto heel proclivity more than as a sound barrier. Derek stepped aside and motioned for the security guard to join them in their listening line in front of Veronica.

More like a firing line.

Jay didn't bother to turn to meet the no-neck he assumed had entered Veronica's inner sanctum. Not for a nanosecond did he believe the Mack CEO had hired out her security. Everything Veronica did was smoke and mirrors. His bodyguard was probably the errant son of one of the syndicate's associates. Someone who'd never snitch and would put a bullet between Jay's eyes upon Veronica's order with zero hesitation.

"Welcome to Mack, Wil." Veronica nodded to the figure Jay saw in his peripheral vision as they stepped to stand in between him and Derek. But not before the scent of roses drenched with spring rain reached his nostrils. For the second time this morning, a very un-autumnal scent filled his senses, tightening his gut.

You're losing it. One glance at an attractive—okay,

blazing-hot—body at breakfast and it had somehow put a curse on him.

"Thank you, ma'am. Cascade Confidential is glad to be of service. So you're my assignment?" The soft-spoken yet assured words did not come from the bulldog muscle man that Jay expected.

What the actual...

He turned and faced the woman standing to his right. She was more than half a foot shorter than his six foot one, had red hair streaked with peach strands that reminded him of the first rays of light at dawn, and while he only saw her profile, it was fair to assume the other side of her was as beautiful as the one he stared at.

The same one he'd sat next to through his maple-bacon waffle meal.

Holy hell's bells, what was going on here? Jay had no problem with women. He and his brother had been raised by a strong mother. He fully supported women in any role on earth, had worked with his share of female FBI agents—who, in his opinion, often outperformed their male peers. They had to, to break through the barriers that still existed no matter how cleverly disguised.

Give her a chance. Somehow his conscience caught up to him before he said something stupid. And costly. *Keep your cover.*

"Wil? What's that short for?" He forced the words through his mouth, still frozen open as he tried not to gawk at the woman who'd finally turned her gaze on him.

Was he the only one in the room who heard, albeit barely, the swift indrawn breath? As she was directly facing him, he knew he was the only observer of her pupils, which contracted before widening as recognition dawned. Her mouth opened, then closed, and she hid her reaction with a polite smile. But she didn't break eye contact. He definitely should, but it was as if she were an electromagnet and he was but an iron filing.

Her eyes alone were enough to bring a man to his knees, or dream of her going to hers for him. Darkest hazel with flecks of gold and green, so reminiscent of the deciduous trees that were turning the Cascade Mountains aflame as fall set in. Unlike this morning, when her hair had been in a ponytail, it was now flowing over her shoulders. His fingers twitched, and he balled his fists.

You're never running your fingers through that silk. Snap out of it, man.

"It's Wil with one *l*. Short for Willow." Either she didn't recognize him, which he knew she did, or she'd decided, like him, to not mention it. At his silence, she pressed. "You know, the tree?" Definitely no-nonsense. The glimmer of a sense of humor. And perfectly imperfect full lips, with that curious scar on the upper one.

Jay swallowed against the deep groan that rumbled silently in his chest.

"You're representing your security company, then? Here ahead of the actual bodyguard?" Derek craned his neck around, looking for the "actual" bodyguard. "No offense, but we're pretty big targets." Always his own best audience, Derek guffawed while no one else paid attention. For once Jay was grateful for the idiot's antics. He needed a heartbeat to regroup, figure out how he'd be able to use Willow O'Malley to his best interest.

"No, our CEO, and headquarters, are located in Seattle. I'm in charge of the Coeur d'Alene office and happen to have a personal protection background. I'll be your bodyguard this weekend." She smiled at Derek.

Maybe Veronica really had hired outside of the company. But if this was true, then she was indeed expecting a major shakeup.

More like shakedown.

Whether the showdown was going to be with the source of their fentanyl in the form of a cartel, or from a rival syndicate, Jay hadn't figured it out yet.

"Not *his* bodyguard. Derek can protect himself." Veronica interjected. "His." She raised her voice at the last and pointed at Jay. Somewhere in his mind it registered again that Veronica was deeply concerned about whatever reason she'd hired a personal bodyguard for her head number cruncher. The CEO and crime syndicate boss was a woman of few words and fewer physical gestures. She usually raised an eyebrow or nodded in response to Derek's pedantic queries. This was a glimpse of another side of the vicious crime boss he knew Veronica to be. Jay would hash this new intel out later, in privacy.

"Again, Veronica, there's no need for Jay here to have a bodyguard. Like I said, I always carry my gun." Derek didn't like this situation any more than Jay. Interesting.

"You're Jay's supervisor in the office, not a 24-7 bodyguard. You're also not my top accountant, who has been targeted by name already." Veronica's impatience reflected in her admonishing tone, which reminded Jay of how a hawk used its talons to shred its prey.

Jay knew he was a decent agent, and his boss had confessed he was the best undercover agent he'd ever worked with. He credited his success to date from his powers of observation and his ability to blend in as needed. To not stick out and draw attention to what he was doing. But with the sudden appearance of Willow O'Malley, it was all he could do to keep his focus in the room instead of on the emotions roiling in his midsection.

Because as he'd stared into the depths of Willow-like-the-tree O'Malley's eyes, his bottom had fallen out. He wasn't a Neanderthal and knew himself well. He recognized his reaction for what it was. Temporary. Fleeting, even. But this woman he'd known for only fifteen seconds, tops, was triggering several emotions in a way he'd never experienced before. At least not all at once. Tight, hot sexual attraction, curiosity, longing—and fear. Jay could dismiss the first three as simple chemistry, biology, whatever. But fear?

Crap. That meant he was threatened by Willow. It wasn't her stature, or the weapon she must be carrying, or whatever bodyguard skills she claimed to have. He didn't know what the hell this had to do with his emotional reaction to a virtual stranger, and he knew better than most that a successful operation wasn't achieved with personal feelings running amok. Even something as easily recognized as lust, desire. *Longing.*

This case had taken a deadly turn for Jay, and it had nothing to do with crime.

Chapter 4

Wil thought she'd seen it all during her two decades in the Corps, which included one combat and several overseas deployments. But as she stood in between two men who were, in her estimation, polar opposites, she accepted that this was a first.

Running into the same man twice in one day was odd, but it happened. What she wasn't used to was seeing the same person again but from such a different perspective. Gone was the sexy, athletic runner she'd sat next to at the diner counter. In fact, if it weren't for his eyes, she might have not recognized him. But it was the same man. She'd remembered the depths of his midnight-blue eyes, the way they sparked with recognition, awareness…desire?

Stop. This was ridiculous. She was just being triggered by the newness of working security as a civilian, out of her comfort zone of cold cases and cybercrime. Forcing herself to refocus, she quickly made a mental assessment of her situation.

The dude who seemed to think he was in charge of everyone except his CEO was a total dork. He'd underestimated her before he'd read her résumé, found out more about her background. No winning points for him.

On the other hand, Veronica Clayton clearly had done

her homework and seemed pleased if not relieved to have a security expert on her team. Wil would have appreciated it more if she'd taken an instant liking to the CEO, if the woman hadn't immediately raised her hackles. What was it about her that reminded Wil of someone else? She'd have to think about it later. Maybe Veronica reminded her of a previous commander or colleague, an unsavory one. Something about this CEO bothered her, but she couldn't put her finger on it. Not yet.

You see a mystery in every situation. Maybe she did. Would she have been more accepting of Veronica if the CEO was instead a colonel or general in uniform, to whom she reported?

It was hard to trust anyone in a position of authority over her who wasn't in uniform when she'd spent countless hours amounting to years ferreting out the worst of the worst in terms of cybercrimes. She couldn't blame Mack's CEO for her own misgivings.

Face it, it's not Veronica Clayton who's got your goat.

When she and Jay had locked gazes, for that split second after she recognized him, she forgot that she was protecting him for the next seventy-two or more hours, forgot that she was here in a professional capacity. Heck, she'd even ignored Veronica Clayton, the woman who'd given CC such a lucrative contract on short notice. For a reason inexplicable to Wil, Jay had sent first a bolt and then several aftershocks of awareness through her. She sure as sunshine wasn't a stranger to sexual attraction and was even friendlier with intimate satisfaction. When it involved zero strings, Wil enjoyed a healthy expenditure of energy with another consenting adult. For the last two decades she'd been surrounded by eligible partners at the peak of their physical acumen, and had enjoyed two longish-term relationships.

Both had ended when she'd been transferred to a different base and long-distance proved too much. Which for her meant it wasn't the right man. She'd be willing to request a change of duty station for someone she felt was her life partner. A partner who had never shown up.

Chiseled handsome wasn't a necessary requirement, nor was overt sexiness. Kindness, a sense of humor and preferably an inquisitive mind that matched hers were her top three sexy-time triggers.

Jay had exhibited none of the above except, maybe, a spark of humor in his gaze, and yet her private parts were shimmy-shaking. First, his suit was ill-fitted and he actually hunched over, *stooped.* She doubted the man had ever lifted a hand weight. His crumpled tie, the knot a far cry from its perfect status this morning, and thick-lensed glasses—circa twenty years ago—were further giveaways to a life spent in front of a computer, far from the outdoors she cherished.

"Do you have any questions right now, Wil?" Veronica's query broke through her most unprofessional musings. *Get a grip, girl. Stay the course.*

"No, thank you. I'll need to familiarize myself with the entire building before I—"

"Employees stay in their assigned office spaces at Mack. It keeps things more streamlined, calmer." Derek spoke up, actually sounding intelligent for the first time since she'd shook his clammy hand. "You're only protecting Jay here, no one else. He's your main man."

Wil fought to keep from clenching her jaw.

"Derek's right, Wil." Veronica's tone had taken on a layer of frost. "You're to stick to Jay's desk area, on this side of the building only. He's your only concern." The hairs on Wil's nape prickled against her collar, and the extra layer of her leather jacket over her white dress shirt wasn't enough to keep the chill off her skin. The air in the office thickened with uncertainty. Was she being threatened?

"Forgive my boldness, Ms. Clayton, but you hired me to protect one of your top assets. I can't do that if I don't have complete access to the very building and areas a potential threat could breach. I don't need to spend a lot of time in any particular office or room. What I'm looking for are all possible ingress and egress paths. Mostly so that, if need be, I can get Jay out of here. A blueprint or diagram of the building would be helpful, too." She held her breath for a split second. Veronica appeared to be considering her argument.

"I think that's hired-security-guard talk for she didn't get us the first time, boss." Derek's grin was one Wil wished she could remove with a quick retort—aka the blue streak she'd learned in the Corps—but her loyalty to her family's business kept her baser instincts quiet.

For now. She bit the inside of her cheek to keep a smirk off her face, offering her best neutral smile.

"I did hear you, and I understand your concerns. I'm not interested in the actual goings-on of your company, Ms. Clayton. I only need to make a visual inspection of the building, identify all the exits and entryways."

Veronica's gaze never wavered, but Wil had the horrifying sense that the woman would slap her if she could. Had she misstepped? No, she was certain she hadn't. Not if she was expected to do the job she'd been hired for.

"So, do I have your permission to do a walkthrough, Ms. Clayton?" she pressed.

Veronica blinked, and her eyelashes—so long and perfectly curled that they had to be fake—moved in what had to be a purposeful motion.

"Excuse me?" Softly spoken, barely above a whisper, Veronica hissed the words through crimson lips. Wil heard the sharp intake of Derek's breath, sensed more than saw her charge, Jay, shift on his feet.

Way to go, O'Malley. She'd gone and ticked off her new employer before she'd been here a half hour.

Wil dug for a modicum of an apologetic tone, reminding herself to keep Toni's and CC's needs at the forefront. They needed this contract or Toni wouldn't have taken her off the cold case and cybercrimes.

"I'm not looking to get off on the wrong foot. I'm ex-military, and my training mandates total situational awareness. I'm not at all interested in whatever your employees are doing unless it involves the safety of Mr. Jones." She looked at Jay. "As long as I'm assigned to protect you, you're my mission."

Jay met her gaze with bland equanimity but she didn't miss the quick tightening of his jaw. Was he holding back laughter or, like Derek, more worried about Veronica Clayton's ire?

She broke eye contact and looked past his shoulder at Derek, who'd gone pastier than she'd have guessed possible.

You've messed up this time.

She turned back to Veronica and readied herself to take the heat. She'd never been fired before, never been reprimanded in the Corps. Toni was going to be so angry—

"Point taken. We're on the same page, Wil, and you obviously deserve the recommendation I received from a colleague to use Cascade Confidential." Veronica stood. "Derek, take Wil around the facility and give her the codes for each of the entrances."

"You mean enable her fob, right?" Derek's cheeks looked like a grandmother had pinched them. He was telling Wil more than he realized. For certain she knew he had little to no understanding of Mack's security system, at least not on a technical level. If the power went out or worse, if the security system got hacked, no one would gain entrance to the building without the codes for the manual cipher locks.

"No, I mean exactly what I said." Veronica's cool demeanor returned, this time with an air of distraction. A CEO had a lot to do in their long day. At least, that's what Wil had observed with all of the senior officers she'd worked under. As a senior enlisted Marine in charge of several dozen persons, she'd found her days nonstop. Right now she was a blip on Veronica's lengthy plan of the day.

"Got it, boss." Derek was back, walking Veronica's hard line. If he was going to argue the point further with his boss, it would be out of the earshot of a mere contract bodyguard.

The three of them left the office together, and Wil recognized an unusual mix of emotions making her stomach roil. Two were familiar enough: gratitude for her Marine training and the backing of Cascade Confidential. Relief that she hadn't been fired on the spot before she'd even begun. But it was suspicious that Mack Manufacturing & Logging might not be totally on the up and up that added an ugly twist.

That's not all.

Truth. What mystified her, annoyed her to heck and back, was the unmistakable sexual awareness her body had felt as she stood next to Jay, who didn't look at all like the man she'd met this morning. Had the diner been that dark, was her need for a healthy sex life that dire that she'd seen what she'd wanted to, what her fantasies would create, instead of reality?

Dang.

"I'll give you fifteen minutes to look around, then you need to be back at Jay's desk, got it?" Derek motioned at the door that led to the other side of the building. Veronica's office suite was in the center, and Wil had only seen the side with the bay of cubicles, a break room and the restroom area.

"I doubt I'll need that long." She pushed through the glass doors before Jay could respond.

In truth, Wil planned to observe a whole lot more and include it in a detailed report for CC eyes only. Unless she discovered activity that required notifying local law enforcement. Something was off here, and it wasn't just her teenage crush, insta-lust reaction to Jay the number cruncher. Maybe it was her cybercrime background, or the fact she was working on a decades-old cold case, that made her suspicious. She hoped this was the case. Because Mack and its CEO hadn't impressed her enough to set off her internal alarm bells.

Had the Cascade Confidential staff done its due diligence in vetting Mack before sending her out here?

Doubt tickled the base of her skull. Not full-on warning. Not yet.

Toni was overwhelmed with the influx of business to the agency; how deeply had she looked into Mack before sending Wil out here? Besides keeping Jay under protection, did she need to worry about her own well-being?

Chapter 5

"How long have you worked here?" Wil spoke to Jay's back. He'd all but ignored her since returning to his cubicle, glancing at her only to make sure she had enough room to maneuver her chair at the L-shaped desk. She faced him instead of the tabletop, which made for a much smaller space between them.

"Huh? Oh, uh, just a few weeks. Less than a month." Jay didn't turn around, intent on the spreadsheets displayed on two of the three mega screens that were mounted over his desk. The third screen showed CNBC, the financial streaming network. The constant stream of data on the ticker had never interested Wil. She couldn't help but smile in her obscure corner of the cubicle. Of course investments and the stock market didn't interest her. If she were about becoming wealthy, she'd never have enlisted, and she wouldn't be working for her family. Sure, both provided decent, even outstanding, incomes, especially when one took all the benefits like health care and pension plans into account. Cascade Confidential's salary was fifty percent higher than what she'd made in the Corps. But Wil wasn't about financial gain, not once her basic necessities were taken care of. Whatever she did had to mean something deeper to her. She needed an altruistic motive.

Maybe that's what was bugging her about Veronica Clayton. The woman was a CEO, and apparently competent. In Wil's experience, good leadership included caring for one's employees. But the way Veronica kept the workers all sealed off in their individual sections, expecting them to eat at their desks, seemed a little stringent. There were break rooms in each section but no chairs or tables to hang out at. Veronica must care for her employees, though, or she wouldn't be concerned enough to hire a bodyguard for her accountant, would she?

Not a question she felt she could ask Jay. Not yet, at least. And definitely not in such an open bay of cubicles, where words carried.

"Where did you work before?"

Silence.

The tedium of pulling words from this nerd wasn't Wil's idea of a fun time. She shifted in her seat, leaned forward. Wil could dismantle, clean and reassemble a sharpshooter's rifle—blindfolded. Sitting at a computer for eighteen-hour days in order to catch crime in the act was also one of her prized skills. Tedious was no problem for her, no matter how much she preferred engaging conversation. A sigh escaped her lips, though, as she stood and stretched her arms overhead. Staying alert was paramount to any security op.

Jay's hand stilled atop the wireless trackpad, as if he sensed her movement and how it had closed the already small distance between them. The white tail of his dress shirt undulated with what she was pretty certain was his spine straightening somewhere under the way-too-big garment. He clearly didn't have a girlfriend to help him dress more attractively.

Wil's arms fell to her sides and she sat back down.

Where the heck had that come from? First, whether Jay

had a romantic partner or not had absolutely zip to do with her—or, more importantly, her job.

"Here and there." The words came out like a soft growl as he pulled his chair closer to his desk. So he *had* heard her, and noticed she was closer.

"You clearly don't like small talk and you're trying to work. I get it, believe me. But we're going to be spending a lot of time together this weekend, and I've found it helps to know a bit about each other so that you'll be more comfortable. This can't be something you're used to, having personal protection." She made an effort to keep her voice low, quiet.

As he turned to look at her, she saw again the blankness, the complete disinterest in his slack jaw, his even brow. Except…his eyes. It was less than a second, but she caught that knowing glint again. Was he aware of doing that? Or did he think he had her fooled?

"Am I used to having my own bodyguard? No, not at all. And you're right. It's not an experience I've ever had." Said with conviction.

"Do you live alone or with a…spouse? Partner?" She was asking purely for professional reasons, of course, in case she'd actually be protecting more than Jay. *Keep telling yourself that.*

"I'm single, Wil, and I live alone." He said her name with the same level of disinterest he'd given her so far. Which was why he surprised her when he tilted his head, made more prolonged direct eye contact. "What made you want to do this for a living?" No curiosity on his part about her relationship status. Her gut dipped, as did her attitude. It had to be from the adrenaline of being on a new job, not disappointment at his lack of interest.

"The usual reasons, I suppose." *Tread lightly.* Her near-miss with Veronica remained uppermost in her mind. She'd counted fifty employees in this one large room, all separated by cubicle walls with no attempt at giving each employee their privacy. Voices carried, and she didn't trust the conversation to stay between them. Plus, there was no telling when Derek would show up again. It wouldn't surprise her if he was crouched on the other side of the upholstered wall.

"Define 'usual.'" Finally, she'd hooked him into dialogue.

"I've always worked in security of one type or another." She didn't want to openly admit she was a cybersecurity expert. It wasn't anything Jay needed to know, and definitely none of the Mack employees needed the information. "My family owns and runs Cascade Confidential, a private security firm, so it was a natural fit for me after my time in the military." He didn't need to know that she'd never actually served as a bodyguard, or that she'd been working for CC for only six months. Or that when she said *security* her experience was almost entirely cyber. As in, not in-person.

"That makes sense." He turned back to his work, then stopped. "Wait, you're protecting me on these premises only, correct? At work? Any threats I'm aware of have been aimed at employees while they're in this office building, not at their residence."

"I'm afraid you're not getting off that easily." She smiled. "I'll be with you twenty-four/seven, until the threat is gone." *Or sooner.* She said a silent prayer that Toni wouldn't have a problem filling this contract with a different person. She still couldn't put her finger on it, but something wasn't right here. But was it Veronica's reminding her of someone she'd worked for, or Jay's contradictory behavior between this morning and now?

She really didn't want to know what Jay's—or Mack's—deal was. She was here to work, and she needed to stay in her lane. Except the man she'd connected with this morning, no matter how briefly, had seemed approachable, intelligent, real. And yes, attractive as all get-out. He'd allowed a sliver of that same energy to break through his accountant persona.

Normally Wil would let all of this go, but after meeting Veronica Clayton and having her warning bells go off the same way they did when she came upon a cybercriminal, she had no choice. She had to rely on her gut.

Which meant she was going to do whatever digging she had to while she was here.

Chapter 6

Jay released a long, slow breath after he was certain Willow was out of earshot.

This was so not good, not what he'd expected. There were surprises with every takedown plan, sure. But having someone as astute, intuitive and, he had to admit, incredibly attractive this close to him right as the Mack manure was about to hit one of their warehouse's ginormous turbo-engine fans, well, this hadn't been something he could have predicted.

It was no different than being watched by Derek. He'd been under no illusion that Veronica's right-hand lackey was monitoring his every move. So why couldn't he shake off his concern over Willow O'Malley?

Probably because he'd seen the knowing green glints in her hazel eyes. She suspected something was going on here. It wasn't hard to see that Veronica didn't fit the stereotype or even the expectation one could have for a logging industry boss. It would take less than a three-minute conversation at the break room counter with one of the many disgruntled employees for Willow to figure out how abruptly Cal had been replaced by his wife, whom many suspected of being in it for the millions, period. She'd let so many employees go—fired them—for nothing more than challenging her poor decisions.

His last thought got him to his feet, grabbing his empty coffee mug and heading for the break room. Jay was conscious of interested gazes, and not because they were from single employees like himself. He'd garnered a bit of a reputation as a good listener since reporting here. Which was exactly what he wanted.

"First break today, eh?" Catherine Porter, a devout Mack employee of several decades, nudged him with her elbow. "Remember what I told you on your first day. No one is paying you overtime for stressing."

"Or for anything else, because I'm salaried."

Catherine chuckled and pulled a pumpkin spice–flavored creamer from the refrigerator. "You got that right, Mr. Smarty-Pants."

"Sadly, I know it." He pressed the brew button on the coffee maker and waited as the aroma from his single pod broke through the stale break room air.

"I saw you have a new friend working with you? Is she a trainee?" It was common knowledge that they were short in many departments, but none more than accounting and finance. What wasn't known to anyone but Jay and Veronica was the reason—Veronica wanted her books cooked not just for the IRS but for whichever other crime syndicate she was planning a merger with.

"Naw, it's part of the extra security we were all promised." He waited for Catherine's reaction.

"Well, if that doesn't top it all." She selected a coffee pod and watched Jay remove his full mug and pod from the machine. "We've all been threatened, if that bomb scare last week was any indication. And what about the tire slashing that's been going on since May?" She shook her head, placed her mug where Jay's had been. "Figures that she'd worry most about her cash."

"They've put in that new security system, all the new cameras, right?" Jay knew very well that the increase in cameras meant nothing unless they were connected and monitored. His team had successfully hacked into the two-bit system last month and discovered that only one-third of the cameras were online. Meaning the vast majority of them positioned about the main office building, the new recreation facility and the three warehouses were dummies.

Catherine snorted. "We need more bodies in security uniforms, if you ask me. I tell you, nothing's been the same since Mr. Clayton got sick." Her voice hitched and she blinked rapidly. "I loved being his secretary, or executive assistant, as the kids say." She waved a plump hand in the air. "No matter now. I'll be retiring at the end of the year."

"How many years will you have been here?" Jay genuinely liked talking to Catherine. And liked the insider information she unknowingly gave to the FBI. Every tiny piece of the puzzle mattered when it came to dismantling such a large, wide-reaching syndicate. Which was about to get bigger.

"Forty." At his look of surprise, she laughed. "Honey, I could be your grandma, biologically speaking. And the stories I could tell you about this place. Did you know it started in a trailer smaller than a double-wide? I had an electric typewriter—trust me, that was fancy for then—and we used a space heater to keep from freezing our tushes off."

"So you always did the admin work for Cal?"

"More than that." She took a step closer, motioned for him to do the same. "I did your job, back when Cal operated in all cash. And you know what? He still preferred cash, even as recently as ten years ago. His boys, Fred and Toby, convinced him to put some of the money into the bank, so to speak."

"Huh." Jay tried to seem interested without being too in-vested. Unbeknownst to her, Catherine had just confirmed what he already knew. And her testimony would definitely help when Cal's two sons from his first marriage were rounded up and on trial for crimes that would send them away for good.

"You thought I was going to tell you that we had a pas-sionate affair, didn't you?" Catherine giggled. "Don't bother denying it. It's written all over your face." She wiped her eyes with a paper napkin she'd pulled from the utilitarian wall dispenser. "No, Cal Clayton was nothing if not loyal to his first wife, Melanie."

"Did she work in the business?"

"After a time, yes, once his two boys were in school." Catherine's tone turned stern. "After she died, ten years ago, Cal was lost. I wondered if he'd retire. He certainly was old enough."

"Why didn't he? I sure would have." Jay gave a quick glance at the wall clock. He'd been talking to Catherine long enough that Derek might ask what they'd been talk-ing about. He didn't want to throw any shade on the long-term and loyal employee. *And future FBI witness.* If all went well.

She sniffed, sipped at her creamer-with-coffee drink. "She convinced him to keep going. That last year, when he could have been off enjoying himself, instead he was here. And there's more." She looked around before leaning in. It was still the two of them.

"Oh?" Jay asked.

"There's a secret room off the office. It's not a secret to any of us who worked closely with Cal, and I'm sure Veronica is using it. Probably for storage, or to change in and out of her over-the-top couture outfits." She leaned back in mock surprise. "What, you think us country folk don't know the difference between off-the-rack and flown in from Paris?" She smiled before turning serious again. "What little Miss Fashionista doesn't know is that Cal kept records in the form of paper files in another secret room. I'll bet my bottom dollar he never told Veronica about that one. A man needs to keep some things to himself. And his personal secretary. Fred and Toby probably know about the papers, too, but they'd never tell Veronica. They don't have any love for her, that's for sure."

Jay held his breath, waited for Catherine to go on, tell him where the other storage area was. He already knew there was no love lost between the sons and Veronica. But as he stared at her, her eyes shifted over his shoulder and the blinds came down in her gaze.

"Hey, J-man, you want to bring the coffee maker over to your desk?" Derek's voice was chipper enough, but he wasn't fooling Jay. Had he heard anything Catherine had said?

"I'd best be back at it myself." Catherine nodded at Jay and completely ignored Derek as she left the break room. *No love lost there.*

"Do you need something from me?" Jay knew he was pushing the boundaries of being a meek accountant.

"Nope, but as always, you need to be prepared for when the boss needs your comfort."

"Comfort?"

"Hey, you know how CEOs are. Their bankroll is their favorite pet. They need to bring it out and stroke it, often."

And the evidence we need to put them away.

"Wil, you okay? How's it going at Mack?" Toni had answered after a single ring, and she sounded as frenetic as she had earlier.

"I'm fine." *Kind of.* "Please don't take this as me throwing shade, but I have to know something, sis. How closely did you look at this company, Mack, before you agreed to take the contract?"

Wil leaned against the hood of her SUV, staring across the employee parking lot at the entrance that led directly into the bullpen of cubicles where Jay worked. "Did Denice find out anything I should know about?" Denice was Cascade Confidential's librarian and case researcher. "I know you're swamped, sis. But please tell me you vetted someone who offered so much for a short-notice contract."

"Hang on." Keyboard clicks sounded over the connection. "I'm pulling up our operational assignments now. Normally I wait to hear back from Denice before signing on a new case, but she's been filling in as Kevin's assistant. He's in charge of running the festival security until midnight Sunday." Kevin O'Malley, at thirty, was one of their two younger brothers and had been a Seattle PD officer until he left to join CC a few years ago. Toni's forceful sigh echoed in Wil's earpiece. "I'm sorry, Wil. I messed up. I didn't cc Denice on the last email, the one that confirmed we'd taken the contract. My bad."

"Well, can you have her do some digging now? I'll do what I can on my end, but this guy isn't the world's best communicator." She suspected she'd have time to dig out all she could about Mack tonight, when she wasn't patrolling around Jay's place. Between her phone, laptop and CC's secure communications, she'd just have to run her own background check. "I don't even know if he lives in an apartment, a house or a cave."

"I'm sorry, Wil. I really dropped the ball here. I promise it's not how I usually do things."

Wil's chest tightened and she swallowed. "It's just as

much on me. I should have asked you about it when you called. It never crossed my mind, to be honest, and it should have. Jay's not the easiest man to get talking about himself." Wil was determined to be a good teammate to her family business, but the painful attempt at drawing Jay out of his snapping-turtle shell had found her searching for something else to focus on.

The memory of how his eyes had sparked with knowing, as if telegraphing he wasn't who he seemed, fueled her curiosity. And reignited her initial reaction to him, in the diner.

Desire.

"This isn't on you, Wil." Toni's reply brought her out of her most dangerous thoughts, thank goodness. "You're right. I was happy to land such a lucrative, short-term bid. But more importantly? I knew you could handle whatever I threw at you and I didn't think twice about it."

"Let's agree to keep each other honest and double-check all future cases you assign me." Wil was used to checklists and backups, both as a former Marine and as a cybersecurity expert. With the complexity of the cyberworld, her checklists had to be created by a trusted software that she'd programmed herself.

"I'll have Denice send you anything she finds ASAP." Toni paused. Wil's nape tingled. "Hang on a minute, sis. Why are you asking all of this, several hours in? Do you have trouble already?"

Wil's gut tightened, not at Toni's tone but at a deeply seared memory. Every family had its old stories, some hilarious and some...not so much. As a teen Wil had gotten herself into scrape after scrape, not because she was a delinquent but because she had no problem sticking up for friends who were being bullied. Her parents had been invited into the high school principal's office on no fewer than a half dozen occasions. Everyone had been relieved when Wil had narrowly missed being suspended right before graduation. She walked to get her honors diploma, in person. Contrary to her confrontational behavior, her grades had been off the charts and she'd been accepted into no fewer than three prestigious universities. But more in alignment with her strong independent streak—and to her siblings' shock and her parents' reluctant acceptance— she'd promptly enlisted in the Marine Corps and was off to Parris Island before summer's end.

That had been over twenty years ago, but Toni's choice of words still triggered Wil today.

"You make it sound as though I'm the cause of any trouble I'd find here, sis. And, for the record, there isn't any. Not yet, that is. I've got a hunch that there's more to Mack than their public business profile. I'm probably way off, but—"

"Don't take this wrong, sis, but are you safe?" Toni interrupted, cutting to the most important line in the Cascade Confidential mission statement. *The safety of our patrons and employees is our top priority.*

Toni oversaw myriad high-risk assignments that CC took on. From what Wil had heard over the years and had seen since returning home, nothing surprised Toni. As CC's CEO, she never underestimated the potential for lethal danger, either.

"Yes, I'm safe, absolutely. And no offense taken. I get it." She did, in fact, get it. The first measure of strength in combat was knowing your limitations. "Are you doing okay, Toni? I mean, I know work is insane, but is there something else?" Wil's heart constricted for all the responsibilities Toni carried on her shoulders. The biggest one being that of her daughter and Wil's beloved niece, twelve-year-old Sierra. While Sierra visited her globe-trotting Foreign

Service Officer father often, Toni was her primary care-giver. Wil was no expert in raising kids, but she wouldn't want to be in Toni's shoes.

"No, nothing else. Sierra's fine. Of course, she's still moping a bit, missing her dad."

"Well, that's normal, isn't it? She spent all summer with him." Wil immediately bit her tongue. Toni had been absolutely miserable without Sierra's vibrant energy filling her craftsman home in Seattle. It didn't seem fair that when Toni could finally be happy that Sierra was back in the nest, the preteen was being surly with her mom.

"Yeah, I suppose so. I could do without the hormonal attitude at times, but it's all part of it." Toni sounded distracted, and Wil knew she was keeping her from countless tasks.

"No frets about me, sis—if it goes south, be assured I'll sound the alarm without hesitation. You've given me plenty of resources to contact you." All CC personnel carried spare burner phones, just in case. As one of the department VPs, Wil also had a secure comms unit that she kept in a kit in her vehicle. Just in case.

"Make sure you do. Reach out for help, that is. I've just texted Denice, and I'll get a hold of Kevin now and see if he's ever heard of Mack Logging & Manufacturing."

"Thanks. Look, I'd better get back inside. I've already had eyes off my charge for too long." But she'd kept her focus on the only exit she'd told him he could use, and she understood the back doors to be locked mechanically as well as electronically, the employees only using the two front exits that were in her line of vision.

"I'm glad you called, Willow." Toni's sincerity and use of her full name—not usual—made Wil need to blink tears away. She'd been more emotional than she ever remembered since returning to the family fold. It was a combination of relief and consolation, as well as her grief at leaving the Corps. Because she was sad to have left before she passed the twenty-year mark and would have received another promotion. But her family needed her more than she'd needed the career recognition.

"I'm glad I called, too."

They disconnected. This brief time outside and away from Jay was worth it to be able to talk to Toni privately about Mack. She did a complete 360, surveying the corporate property as she'd done when she'd first arrived. It was certainly remote enough that any threat wouldn't be random. Veronica had made it clear that she was only worried about "disgruntled employees" and not so much concerned over environmental protesters.

But a security threat was a threat, no matter what flag they waved. This front entrance was secure, though. No one was getting in unless permitted. Wil wasn't a forensics expert, but she'd bet the extra-thick glass on the doors and windows that faced the parking lot was bulletproof, same as her CC SUV windshield and frame.

Mack Logging & Manufacturing had been built as a fortress.

No, no one was getting in who didn't have the right codes and the latest security chip on their ID badge. Veronica had mentioned that while she'd been the one to terminate any employees who'd issued threats to the company, it was pure coincidence that they were the same ones threatening the company today. But she must think that there were still inside threats, otherwise why hire a personal bodyguard? For a numbers guy?

Her suspicions would have to wait to be appeased until either she had time to do some internet digging or Denice or

Kevin discovered or knew offhand about something sinister about Mack. Wil wasn't a stranger to misguided intuition, though. She knew that waiting for the facts was important, and that feelings, no matter how visceral, weren't facts.

As Wil walked back toward the entrance, though, she couldn't shake the shadow of apprehension that had plagued her since she'd driven up to Mack's parking lot. Her emotions might not mean something sinister was afoot, but this fact didn't keep a shudder from stalking across her shoulders.

Chapter 7

"What is she staring at? And who did she have to call so urgently that she left Jay's cubicle? She's been on the job all of what, half a day?" Veronica's gaze narrowed on one of the twenty-seven screens that hung on the wall of her secret security closet. Each displayed a different security camera's view of Mack property in full, high-detail color. She'd spared no expense on security since she'd taken over from Cal.

"She probably had to check in with her boss, is all. Or call her boyfriend." Derek stood next to Veronica and fought the impulse to touch her as the scent of her perfume wafted up to his nose and made him hard.

"Well, make sure she doesn't do that too often. Next time, go outside with her and listen. We can't afford another mole."

"Relax. She's fine, and not very sharp. She was trying to figure out what Jay was working on and I could tell it was over her jar head. That's what they call Marines, you know. Jarheads." He laughed. "We have nothing to worry about." He stepped closer.

They were alone in the secret safe room just off her office. She called it her safe closet, but it was actually almost as large as her office, complete with a folding twin cot and

enough food rations to last days if not a solid week. The
door to the safe room was disguised by her office's fancy
built-in shelves that held the coffee bar Veronica rarely
used. She didn't need caffeine and didn't invite business
associates in to drink joe.

"Knock it off, Derek. Don't act like you ever know what
the hell's going on." She turned to him, and her words were
harsh but her eyes were on fire. There was one way and
one way only to calm down Veronica Clayton when she
got knotted up like this. And it was all for him.

"Let me take the edge off, sugar." He reached for her,
but she grabbed him first and stroked him through his trousers. He groaned and lunged for her.

Veronica held up her free hand between them. "No kissing. Don't mess up my makeup or hair." She growled the
command as she bit into his neck. Derek groaned again,
this time in acquiescence. He had no interest in Veronica's
mouth unless it was on him. Sure, she acted all tough boss
lady in front of the others, but alone, she was his. She just
didn't know it yet.

Afterward, Veronica sent Derek back to keep an eye on
the bullpen. Or, as Veronica called it, "the hive." She was
clever, he gave her that. He much preferred working for her
than his former boss. Although he missed the elder Clayton's traditional opinions on women needing to stay in their
place. Poor guy hadn't realized his trophy wife would end
up running the show for him.

Derek approached Jay's desk and paused. He had a few
seconds to take in the scene before either the geek or the
wannabe cop realized they were being observed. Just as
he'd told Veronica, the woman, Wil, was nothing more than
a body with a gun.

Jay was working hard with the accounts, Derek could tell by the focused look of concentration on the accountant's face. Derek was grateful to be an executive type and that he'd been born with the intelligence to handle more important things than the books, like Jay. He honestly didn't get why Veronica was so steamed up over their money tracking. But he appreciated any opportunity to help her blow off that steam.

Blow being the operative word. No other woman had enjoyed putting her mouth on him more than Veronica. He kept his amusement to himself as he walked to Jay's desk.

"You've got an hour left today." He spoke to Jay only. There was no need to address the bodyguard. She was an extra, expendable. He wondered if she knew she'd be the first to go when it all hit the fan. Because J-man was a big target, knowing what he did about the numbers.

"Huh? Oh, okay. Got it." Jay never looked away from his computer displays. Derek snorted. Book-smart people were the worst. Zero street smarts. His own street wisdom had enabled him to climb the ladder at Mack and meet the Clayton family at eye level.

Yeah, the numbers guy was as close to stupid as Derek had ever known. So was his protection. Derek grinned and kept walking. Before any of these dimwits could say boo, he and Veronica would be sitting pretty on top of the largest crime family in North America. Hell, in the world, as far as he was concerned.

Jay groaned silently. It wasn't that he couldn't play the distracted geek. Hell, he'd done and would continue to do whatever he had to for the success of this op. It was more that he wanted to throat punch Derek every time the snide jerk told him what to do.

"What time do you usually go home?" Wil's softly spoken words broke through his thoughts and elicited a fantasy of his mouth against hers...

Stay present.

Keeping his cover was number one. From the company stats he'd been scouring, Mack Logging & Manufacturing had received a multimillion-dollar influx of cash only last week, and another one last month. Veronica was on the move, gobbling up what he assumed were other companies and selling off several of the storefronts that had laundered her money for the past year. The local news last night had reported that several longtime suspected criminal money launderers had sold their business fronts, from nail salons to laundromats. The numbers all matched. Almost too well, in fact. Didn't Veronica know that too perfect was as much a red flag as mistake after mistake?

Had those other criminal syndicates sold their operations willingly, or, more likely, been coerced by Veronica's threats? And when would another criminal organization come calling for retribution?

"What time do you finish?" Sharper this time. His bodyguard was becoming a true thorn in his thoughts. *Not good.*

"I've been staying late, till seven." He mumbled, hoping to limit the exchange. Talk about unfairness. Not only had he been assigned an extra cling-on, but Willow O'Malley was a beautiful woman who wasn't wearing a wedding band.

Crap. Why had he noticed that? *Because you were checking her out and saw how slim and feminine her hands are.*

"Can you take your work home with you? On a laptop?"

So now she was being Bodyguard Obvious.

"As a matter of fact, no. The accounts, and the proprietary software they use, are all exclusive property of Mack.

They don't allow any employees to work remotely." He leaned toward her and spoke quietly, not wanting his words to carry. Derek was like a whack-a-mole. Jay never knew when the lackey would pop his head over the partition.

Jay wasn't looking over his cubicle wall, though. Why would he, when he could drink in Willow's hazel intensity? Her eyes sparked with challenge for the briefest moment, narrowed. Willow straightened and blinked, offered him a self-deprecating smile. "Yeah, that makes sense. Since you're basically holding the purse strings. Sorry about all the questions. You don't need a babysitter or a nanny. I don't have any experience with accounting, so I know my questions are probably very basic. I'm just trying to get a feel for your routine so I can do my job, is all."

Sure you are. Jay turned back to his computer and bit his inside cheek. There was more than one of them faking it here.

Chapter 8

The rest of the workday played out in boring fashion. Save for the sparks Wil experienced every time her gaze met Jay's.

More like collided.

She was happy to get out of the building and head to his home. He'd reluctantly agreed to leave his vehicle in the employee parking lot and allow her to drive him to his residence. The new-car scent of the company SUV was overridden by the scent of sandalwood soap and a more unique scent she attributed to Jay. Her nipples tightened under her lace bra and cotton blouse, and she was grateful that she'd kept her leather coat on. Not that Jay Jones, CPA, would be looking at her breasts. Or would he? She stifled a sigh.

Toni would never let her work outside the office again if she knew Wil was struggling against a most inopportune surge of lust.

No question, she had to get a social life as soon as this stint was over. Maybe she'd cave to the suggestions of her friends—a tight-knit group of four women who'd all enlisted at the same time—and finally download a dating app to her phone. It went against her security training to use any kind of app she didn't absolutely need, but she couldn't afford to let her lack of a sex life affect her job performance. Not that she'd let Jay do that. Not this Jay, anyway.

Now, the man she'd met in the diner…

Wil reminded herself, for the sixth time in the last five minutes, that the man sitting in her SUV's passenger seat was her *charge*, and absolutely not her *type*. Chances were that CC's researcher, Denice, or Wil herself, would dig up some heavy dirt on Mack, find out the corporation wasn't what it seemed. What legit company needed protection solely for their CPA? Veronica may have hired bodyguards for other employees, but from all that Wil saw when she'd walked through the office spaces, she was the only one. Every other employee operated solo in their respective cubicles. She hadn't checked out the warehouses, though. Maybe some of the hands-on loggers and operators were being protected.

"You'll turn left in about another half mile." Jay's smooth voice resonated across the mere feet between them and through her rib cage, causing parts of her to tingle that had no business even being awake while she was on assignment. Annoyance clawed at her composure.

"Thanks." She was surprised that he hadn't questioned her refusal to use either of their phones' GPS systems and had acquiesced to her request to adjust his phone's settings to maximum privacy. Maybe he was resigned to the fact that whatever she said was how it had to be for the foreseeable future. While she couldn't eliminate every potential that he was being tracked, she could minimize it. Of course, when she'd looked at his phone's settings, he'd already been set for bear. When she'd asked about his phone, he'd shrugged and said he'd kept it at factory settings. But factory settings usually allowed for little privacy. Data collection was how companies created algorithms and made money.

Maybe he knows more about digital security than he's letting on.

CC had outfitted Wil's company car with all the technological bells and whistles money could buy.

At first she'd bemoaned having to keep her "baby" parked in her garage and using it only for personal driving. Her pink Jeep Wrangler, complete with a USMC insignia on the tire cover, had seen her through thick and thin over the last decade. But she was more grateful for the SUV's capabilities. CC never skimped on having the best, most up-to-date tools.

Donna O'Malley, her mother and CC's founder, had launched the private business after a short career in the CIA. Family lore was that Donna had met Wil's father during one of her rookie assignments and it was love at first sight. Judging by how quickly thereafter her eldest sibling, Toni, was born, all the O'Malley siblings agreed it had to have been more like lust at first sight.

Donna O'Malley never mentioned her experiences, barely alluded to having ever worked for the agency, but a lot of CC's procedural practices went back to her CIA training. CC specialized in private investigation and larger-scale security operations, though. From what Wil had surmised, Toni usually contracted out personal protection services to reliable experts. Guarding Jay Jones was an anomaly.

Lucky me.

As she drove the target of potential death threats back to his apartment, she was grateful for CC's attention to detail with all things technological. Anything that would prevent her from having to use her weapon was a win in her book.

"Where did you move from?" She sought to keep her voice neutral, to not sound as though she was pumping him for Mack background information.

"Back East."

"New York, Chicago?" she prompted, catching a quick glimpse of his profile. Had it looked so chiseled in his cubicle?

"New York." Grudgingly. "Look, Willow—"

"It's Wil," she corrected him, ignoring how delicious her full name sounded rolling off his tongue. No one called her Willow except those closest to her. And her last serious partner, whom she'd agreed to marry, to settle down with. Until their mission had been blown sideways, literally. She swallowed and fought against the tears that still threatened, five years later. Chris's near-death experience thanks to an IED had triggered a change of heart in her ex. He'd left the military shortly thereafter and taken a completely different path. She'd gotten over the initial shock and subsequent grief at losing a cherished relationship. But she'd kept the lesson learned: Wil did better with short-term relationships.

"Wil." His sigh echoed in the front seat. "I'm not sure why Veronica feels the need to have you protect me at home. I'm totally okay with you dropping me off and then picking me up in the morning. I won't tell if you don't."

"I'm totally *not* okay with that, Jay. No offense, but if this is going to work, you're going to have to trust my judgment with your personal security. Wouldn't you say the same to anyone who questioned your accounting expertise?"

"Apples and oranges," he muttered.

"What's that?" She immediately regretted how sharp her words sounded. Her job was to protect, not reprimand.

"The thing is, Wil, I welcome someone questioning my account management. It keeps me on my toes. I imagine when it comes to security, you have to believe your way is best."

"Something like that, yes." She bit her lip to keep from

saying any more. What she really wanted to say. That she heard the passive-aggressive intention in his reply, and that she was beginning to suspect he and Mack were involved in something more nefarious than Pacific Northwest logging and manufacturing. Better to play it safe, though, and keep the upper hand. Let him think her ignorant.

Jay soaked in Willow's profile from the passenger's seat. Her brilliant red hair deeply contrasted with her creamy skin, as well as the backdrop of browns and greens that the woods provided. She shot him a glance right before she turned onto the mountain road. *Caught.* He looked away.

Willow was a good enough driver, but he couldn't help but tense as she hit the brakes, slowed, flicked on her signal light and made the almost U-turn onto the one road that he'd despised since arriving in Washington State. Because of how it hugged the side of a mountain, the lone shoulder on the right nonexistent, he felt like a caged animal every time he took it home. There was no other road in or out of the property he was staying on.

"Careful." The word escaped him as Willow navigated an S turn, so narrow the drop-off disappeared from his line of sight and made it feel as if they were going to plunge into the deep gorge.

"What, are you afraid I'll send us over the edge?" She gave the wheel a slight jerk and his insides tightened, for the first time since he'd met her not from lust but annoyance.

"That's not freaking funny. You realize there's nothing here to stop us on my side, right?"

Her laughter was robust, full of not humor as much as joy. If they'd met under different circumstances—

No. She's one of them.

"It's only a sheer drop, Jay. Don't worry, at least there

are trees. One of them, or okay, maybe a few, would stop us from going all the way down the side of the mountain."

"I don't want to find—"

With zero warning, a dark-colored vehicle loomed up on Willow's side, occupying the only other—the oncoming—lane. Jay barely made out its profile, as it was slung lower than the SUV. Its windows were tinted black, the occupants invisible.

"Hey, watch it!"

But Willow was ahead of him, downshifting and applying her brakes before his warning was fully formed. When she again shifted, this time into Reverse, she floored the gas pedal so hard the SUV jerked, making his head bang against his headrest.

"Hang on and shut the hell up." She issued the order quickly, as if it were an afterthought. Which it had to be as she obviously had her total attention on driving, keeping them alive as the mystery vehicle made a tight turn in front of them and once again headed for them. But this time, head-on.

"What the hell!" He reached to grab the wheel from her only to have Willow smack him in the nose. Hard.

"I. Know. What. I'm doing." Without missing a maneuver, she shifted from Reverse to Drive and again pressed the accelerator to the max. The engine didn't so much as groan, as its computer board had to be tops in technology with the way it responded.

It was a classic game of chicken, without the clucks. At least not in their vehicle. Willow hugged the mountainside, as did the sports car. Jay wasn't going to let them both die like this. He reached to grab the wheel again, but it was too late. The attack car was less than a second from crashing head-on into them.

Chapter 9

Wil watched the dark late-model sports coupe swerve at the very last moment, its tires squealing to maintain contact with the narrow road. It sped past Jay's side, and if it had greater height it would have ripped off her side-view mirror. Only when its brake lights blinked before making what she knew was a sharp turn a full quarter mile back did Wil allow herself to breathe.

Without preamble she drove back onto the right side of the road and continued as if she hadn't just almost died with her first real, in-person client as a civilian.

"Are you certain your place is only a third of a mile from here?" He might be shaken, have his surroundings mixed up.

"Yes." His clipped response made her cast a quick glance at him. Her knuckles stung at the sight of his bloodied nose.

"There are tissues in the glove box. Sorry about your nose."

He snorted, then groaned. "Good thing there was no one else on the road."

"Did you recognize the car or driver?" she asked.

"No."

She wasn't going to let him know she'd memorized the license plate. "We're not out of the woods yet. I want to make sure they don't come back." But she didn't think whoever had targeted them would risk messing with her again. Not right now, anyhow. If they'd thought Jay's bodyguard was an easy mark, she'd proved them wrong.

Whoever had sent the killer car wouldn't send the same person again. They'd send out a more experienced assassin next time.

"I have to give it to you, Wil. You saved our lives." Grudging acceptance tinged his tone.

"I knew he—or she—wasn't going to hit us head-on. It wouldn't do them any good if they died, too, would it?"

Wil tried to act as if the last thirty seconds were no biggie, when in fact she had never been more grateful for the defensive driving skills she'd picked up in the Marine Corps, refreshed by the advanced course Toni had insisted she take before assuming her role at Cascade Confidential. Without either, she wasn't sure she or Jay would still be here to talk about the near miss. Her reflexes hadn't let her down, and her counteractions had kept them alive. But her heart pounded, fueled by the aftershock of adrenaline.

More than ever, she believed she'd signed up for a lot more than protecting a geeky numbers guy. Just who was Jay Jones?

The unanswered question reminded her that she'd landed in a wasps' nest of trouble with this job. If the bare-bones facts she was trying to piece together weren't enough, she was also damnably drawn to the man who was as dangerous as the driver sent to take them both out.

She remained quiet for the rest of the drive, the silence between them only broken by the quiet *whirr* of the hybrid engine.

Jay's jaw ached from clenching, and it wasn't getting any better as Willow drove them closer and closer to what he had considered his relative safe zone. *Relative* because undercover work was never a safe bet. And until now, his life hadn't been threatened. Now that they'd both almost died at the hands of a killer driver, he had to face facts: No place was safe. Why would Veronica's rivals target him now? Why not take him out sooner, if the showdown he was expecting loomed so close?

He wasn't too stupid to live, either, as his colleagues referred to suspects or agents who made boneheaded decisions in the midst of a lethal situation.

Veronica had unknowingly played an open hand to him when she hired Willow. He was certain their meeting at the diner this morning was not coincidental. The security hire was letting him know he was being watched. Which was why she hadn't said anything about running into him at breakfast when they'd been introduced. It was Veronica's way of letting him know that she was keeping a close eye on him, that she might not buy that he was trustworthy. No matter the long line of vetting he'd taken years to establish for his persona.

Willow wasn't here only to babysit him, to make sure he was who he said he was, but probably also to keep him from being taken by a rival syndicate. The crime bosses and their respective syndicates that his team expected Veronica to go after would want his insight. Either to know the best way to protect themselves from Veronica's planned takeover, or how to go on the offense and destroy the Clayton kingdom before they became absorbed in it.

But that assassin driver wasn't looking to take anyone alive. He or she had wanted *both* Jay and Willow dead.

He was certain Veronica's security detail had vetted him via their crime syndicate connections or he would have never landed this job, wouldn't be in the devil's lair, so to speak. It was a testament to his years undercover—all for this particular op—and the tireless efforts of the entire team back in DC. But no undercover role was infallible. Had Veronica found out he was law enforcement? Had she ordered the hit?

Why not have Willow take him out? A bullet to the head would be a lot neater than driving them off a cliff. And why throw away an asset like Willow, who clearly knew how to survive in this world?

Maybe Willow doesn't work for them. Maybe she's an innocent player. The thought shook him, and not because he thought for a moment it was anything to consider. This had to be the aftershock of almost dying. Of meeting his maker before bringing down the Claytons.

The question he should be asking himself was if the entire scene had been staged. Willow had demonstrated she knew how to handle a driving attack. Was this a way to scare him, get him to open up to her?

"Do you get surprises like that often when you're coming home in the evenings?" Wil asked. Oh, she was smooth, all right.

"No." He played along, knowing he had to keep her on her toes. If he was going to be watching his back with her, he'd make damn sure she wasn't cozy in his presence, either. "By the way, where did you learn those maneuvers? Phew! It's a good thing you were driving. I'm sure I would have had us over the edge after the first turn."

"I binge-watch detective shows." Her deadpan gave him pause, until he looked more closely and saw the edge of her lips twitch, revealing a ghost of a dimple in her right cheek. Her skin was so smooth, and his fingertips itched as he imagined how it would feel.

"Not funny." He shot the retort like a fifth grader and

wished he'd remained silent. A nerd with zero law enforcement experience wouldn't engage. They'd be cowed, maybe even having a panic attack. Inexplicably to him, he couldn't bring himself to play the timid, uninitiated persona in front of her.

"Looks like you're pretty remote up here, Jay," Willow said. "I thought you'd be in one of those last subdivisions we passed."

"I lucked out on a nice piece of acreage and a home with good bones. It's no showcase, let me warn you. Not yet, anyway."

Her sharp glance gave him a brief glimpse of her hazel eyes, the amber glints reflecting the shafts of sunlight cutting through the surrounding woods. His gut flipped and sent instant primal urges to his groin. He forced himself to focus on the road, on what he needed to do to stay alive for the next few days. Sexy or not, he might need to take Willow out before she did him in.

He hadn't been certain that someone from Clayton's syndicate had done much more than a drive-by of the home he'd given them as an address. Now that he'd been attacked on the way home, he needed to tell his team that he was in their crosshairs. But he couldn't pick up and move into a hotel, or another place. It'd raise the red flag with Mack, for sure.

The house was a godsend for him and his team. With cyber–smoke and mirrors, the cousin of a retired agent— who actually owned the house—had been made to look like they'd sold the place to Jay. It was within reach financially for a CPA with the years of experience his fake résumé boasted. Not for most FBI agents, though. And definitely not for Jay, who owned his condo in Northern Virginia, NoVa, not far from headquarters currently located in Washington, D.C. The NoVa area was one of the most expensive in the country, definitely on the Eastern seaboard, and a good chunk of his take-home pay went to his mortgage. He looked at the condo as a long-term investment.

The condo was perfect for his work life, but Jay preferred to spend his free time truly off. He frequently went off-grid to explore state and national parks, to hike for days without having to talk to another person. When it was time to come West for this final leg of his undercover assignment, he'd simply driven his beat-up Dodge camper van onto the thirty-three-acre property in Colbert, Washington, and set up shop. And he'd changed out his legit Virginia license tags for Washington plates, of course.

His real home, his van, was hidden amid the woods that bordered this undercover property. Out of view of the impressive modern home with the winding driveway that Willow drove up and parked her SUV.

"Okay, wow, what a nice place!" Willow's observation reflected the most emotion he'd detected from her since she'd shown up at Mack. She immediately bit her very full bottom lip, leaving a smudge of lipstick on her front tooth, as she stared through the windshield.

Not that he was interested in her lips, her mouth, or licking the pink stain off them, of course. His assessment was purely professional, so that he'd be able to provide a full after-action report to headquarters. *Doesn't matter.* Considering her as a possible target to be eliminated, a threat to the entire mission, proved a better headspace.

"Is it as impressive on the inside?" Willow didn't seem like she was pretending as her gaze took in every detail of the house. He turned his own observation to the midcentury split-level, seeing it through her eyes. What he'd dismissed as a tool to help him get through his ruse was not an inconsequential piece of real estate. The cedar-plank walls were faded but had stood the decades with ease, as had the unique roof that appeared flat but was gently sloped to allow for rain to slough off pine needles and the random leaf. There were few deciduous trees on the immediate half acre surrounding the house, the tree line of the woods beginning only in the back, past the expansive deck—the part of the house he admired second only to the natural forest that embraced it. He would spend his mornings drinking black coffee on the deck, his nights sipping single malt, if it was his home and not a temporary prop for his mission.

"Yeah, it's nice enough. I mean, I'm proud of it, glad I could afford it. But the reason it was in my budget is because it needs a lot of work. I started the rehab before I moved out here, and at least three or four more months of work need to be done before I'll be able to fully use it. I've been living in one or two rooms, tops." That was the story the agency had given him to stick to. The actual owner had decided to use their time away to get a major renovation taken care of. Piles of lumber and several pallets of bathroom and kitchen tile were in the garage, and two of three bedrooms had their carpets torn up. The kitchen was completely unusable, with a cooler and water dispenser its only working "appliances." So the "just in case" story, in the event one of Veronica's thugs—aka Mack employees—checked out his residence, seemed solid. That was before another person was going to actually spend the night here, that was, and have time to take a closer look and figure out that he wasn't living here at all. Which in turn put his current hideaway at risk, his entire operation in peril.

Damn it.

He'd hoped he wouldn't have to show the house to anyone from Mack, at least not on the inside. And he hadn't detected a break-in, not yet.

"I came prepared, if you're worried about me." She said it like she knew he wasn't at all even thinking of her, pointed her thumb at the back of the vehicle. "I've got all the camping gear you can imagine back there, including a sleeping bag, pad and lantern. I can bunk anywhere."

"Oh, so you'll sleep out here, in the back of your car?" Relief crept in. If he didn't have to see her—

"No, that's not a good idea, remember? I need to keep eyes on you, or close enough, until I'm told otherwise."

"Gotcha." He tried to retreat to his undercover nerd persona, tried to keep the aggravation from his tone. "I, ah, appreciate what you're doing." Like hell he did, but he figured a geek with zero self-defense skills would.

"No thanks necessary. It's my job."

He didn't reply, but reached for his door handle. Willow reached out and grabbed his upper arm.

"No!" It was a direct order, but the sharp bite of her tone didn't faze him. The heat of her touch seared straight across his chest and down to his groin. That more than fazed him.

Shit.

He took his hand off the door, placed it on his lap, stared out the windshield. In his peripheral vision he saw Willow shift her seat to face him, resting her arm on the wheel.

"Look, Jay, I get it. It's the pits to have someone, especially a stranger, watching your every move, and more so because you didn't ask for it, your boss did. I've been where you are, back in the military, when I had to operate in combat situations that I hadn't been specifically trained for. As much as I was a fully trained Marine, my expertise isn't in the field as much as the office. I still needed the experts to help me get past some roadblocks, literally."

Do what a real CPA would do. Stay quiet.

"Is it fair to say you've never had any security training

or personal protection before today?" Her softened voice, the gentle question, grated. She wasn't intentionally patronizing, and if he were truly a novice in the world of security, he'd probably appreciate her effort.

"Correct." His jaw tightened.

She nodded. "I'm going to tell it to you straight, just like the Marine who saved my life did. Please listen to me, because your life may depend upon it. There are certain procedures I need you to follow with zero question while we're working together. I'll talk you through all of them." She unbuckled her seat belt. "First being, you never, ever try to grab the steering wheel out of my hands again. Got it?"

"Yes," he lied. And wasn't going to admit that her punch in the nose had thrown him.

"Next, you are to remain in the car until I open your door. This won't change the entire time I'm protecting you, so the sooner you accept it, the easier for both of us. And safest for you."

Man, could he tell Willow a thing or two about what protecting someone entailed. Instead, he forced the dumbass expression onto his face and faced her. He blinked, slowly, as if trying to comprehend her lukewarm attempt at pretending to be a bodyguard.

"That seems…excessive. We're out in the middle of nowhere." The ego he'd thought he'd managed well using the skills he'd acquired from years of fieldwork screamed to be let out. To tell Willow that he knew she wasn't a bodyguard of any kind but in reality a glorified babysitter, a lackey, working for a vicious mob boss.

"Are you questioning my abilities, Jay? Because I assure you I have a solid working knowledge of how to protect someone." The steel glint in her irises sent a shock through him, and this time it wasn't sexual awareness as much as a warning. Had she read his freakin' mind?

He cleared his throat, looked away, stared at the wide garage door's decorative trim. Definitely not his taste. Whoever owned this place for real didn't appreciate clean lines like he did.

Willow has very clean lines.

"Not at all." He coughed, made a show of squirming in the leather seat of the tricked-out SUV. He'd bet his next paycheck that he was looking through a bulletproof windshield. "Do you mind? I drank a lot of coffee today." There. That sounded very nerdy and not at all like a man who was intensely curious about—make that *mystifyingly attracted to*—the woman he spoke to.

"Got it." She quickly exited the car, and Jay used the brief seconds alone to take a deep breath, only exhaling once she'd reached his side of the car. A wave of exhaustion gave him pause.

In the twenty-minute drive from the office to his pseudoresidence, staying undercover had taken more energy than he'd used since reporting to Mack several months ago.

All the more reason to be very, very careful around Willow O'Malley.

Hell, that probably wasn't even her real name.

Chapter 10

"You weren't kidding when you said you were doing some work on the inside. You've all but gutted this place." Willow holstered her weapon, a Sig Sauer pistol. She'd requested that CC pay for it because, unlike the other makes of handguns CC normally provided its agents, she was more familiar with it.

After she texted Toni the license plate of the attack car, she'd completed a thorough check of the house, going room to room and clearing each, just as she'd learned in urban combat training. Which she'd had to use for real once during her Marine career. The compact Sig Sauer pistol seemed like overkill in the nonthreatening environment of Jay's torn-apart house, but looks could be deceiving. Any situation could turn deadly in a blink, just as their drive from Mack to here had. Which reminded her, she needed to check back in with Toni. The house was much larger than it appeared from the road, and the main bathroom a thing of beauty, as was the few other spots where updates had been completed. Once back with him in the kitchen, she mentioned her observations to Jay.

"It was in bad shape when I bought it." He turned away, looked through a kitchen window. As mesmerizing as his profile was to her, even with further circumstantial proof that he was part of something bigger, something sinister, she needed to find out if Toni had dug up more information on the company.

She watched as Jay stepped over to a large cooler and pulled out a sparkling water. "Would you like one?" Jay turned toward her. Without waiting for her reply, he handed her the bottle of water before squatting on his haunches next to a second large cooler. "Or maybe you'd prefer a beer?"

"Water's perfect. On duty. Thanks." She accepted the surprisingly cold bottle and unscrewed it. "Must be some cooler that it keeps your stuff this chilled. How often do you need to replace the ice?" She had a hard time picturing him going to so much effort for his day-to-day living. He seemed fully invested in his job, evidenced by how he'd pored over Mack's account spreadsheets all day.

"Never. It's plugged in." He motioned at the cord she hadn't seen. "The place still has power and running water. No heat, air-conditioning or hot water, though. The ducting is being replaced and the flash water heater hasn't been installed yet."

"It's been a cold fall so far. You must need heavy blankets at night." She all but bit her tongue as the words flew out of her mouth. The last thing she needed was for nerd Jay to think she noticed him as anything other than her current contract. His hair hung low across his brow and its dark curls contrasted sharply with his sapphire eyes as they reflected the half dozen bare bulbs hanging from the ceiling. As he straightened from the cooler, he seemed taller, more of a presence than he had in the office. Why hadn't she noticed how broad his shoulders were in that tiny cubicle?

Heat shot from her breasts to between her legs, and she shook her head, as if the gesture would shake some sense into her. This was so not the time for sexy thoughts, and

Jay was definitely not a candidate for appeasing her hormonal cravings. That's all it was, her neglected need for a decent sex life.

Toni was going to get an earful from her when this contract was fulfilled. It had to be the short notice of the assignment combined with its sudden lethal turn that had her hormones mistaking Jay for a stranger-with-benefits prospect. As if she'd ever swipe right on his profile. They had practically nothing in common. Venturing out to the Pacific Northwest was probably as far as he'd ever been from home, which he'd not even identified, only saying he'd come from "back East."

"I assume you sleep in the main bedroom, the one with what appears to be a brand-new spa bathroom? Nice detail with the blue glass trim tiles, by the way. And it looks like you're already enjoying it. I don't blame you. Have you ever been to Japan?" The bathroom was a classic Japanese steam room with the entire room tiled, not just the floor or part of the walls as with standard US bathrooms. A soaking tub equipped with steam nozzles sat in the middle of the room. It already smelled like sea salt.

"Uh, yeah, that. It…it was the first room to get finished. It's going to be a great way to soak away the aches from sitting in front of a computer all day. But like I said, no hot water yet, so I haven't christened it. And no, I've not been to Japan." His voice was staccato, as if talking to her was a painful exercise he wanted nothing to do with. He shifted on his feet on the stripped kitchen floor like he was preparing to run. She knew he'd just flat-out lied to her, if the faint bathtub ring on the new tub was to be trusted. He'd used the bathroom—why lie about it?

She watched him, pondered her next words. There was no use in confronting him, not yet. Not until she knew exactly who he was and who his allegiance was to. She sure hoped Toni got the information she needed sooner than later.

His skin flushed and she wondered if she were simply being dramatic, reading too much into her gut's tugs. Maybe Jay was absolutely who he said he was: an accountant with more love for figures than anything else. Wil knew she could come off as a ballbuster; it was part and parcel of being a successful Marine. Maybe she was overwhelming him. Maybe the sparks she sensed between them were all from her, or if mutual, maybe he didn't have a lot of experience with real, live women. Didn't nerds spend a lot of time in front of a computer, after all? She wondered how many women he'd ever been alone with. She'd just listened to a podcast about people who didn't lose their virginity until later, well past the usually expected adolescent seasons of high school and college. Was he one of them?

None of your business. Keep your focus on your job.

She shook her head again and caught the look of disbelief on Jay's face. He had to be thinking she was odd herself. And wasn't she? Why the heck had that podcast come to mind now?

As if she were playing out a scene from a television sitcom, a giggle welled up and she swigged more of the carbonated water to disguise it. But her erratic breathing sucked up too much liquid and she began to gasp as tiny bubbles scratched her trachea.

"Wrong pipe?" His Captain Obvious reply made her giggles morph into an all-out belly laugh and she bent over, trying to cough the remaining droplets from her throat while her body shook with the hilarity of the situation. Tears welled and spilled down her cheeks.

"Willow. Seriously. Are you okay?" He took a step toward her.

She straightened to find him standing no more than six inches away, her eyes even with his chest. His arms were lifted at his sides, probably ready to perform the Heimlich maneuver. The thought of his hands touching her skin under her rib cage, of him standing behind her and pulling her up against him, made her freeze. Not from fear or wariness, but from the sheer power of her attraction to him.

The man she'd briefly encountered in the diner had returned. Jay's face didn't resemble a nerdy number cruncher, but a fully capable man. His hands were strong as they reached to grasp her upper arms. His broad knuckles and wrists covered with strands of dark hair that matched the locks falling into his eyes were highlighted in the soft shaft of lingering light coming in from over what she assumed had been the kitchen sink. His hands on her arms forced her to look up, up, into his eyes, to tell him she was okay.

Oh man, his eyes.

Wil couldn't look away from the intensity of his expression. His violently blue irises were down to small rims around his dilated pupils. No sound broke the heavy silence surrounding them save for the wind that seemed to be constant in the Pacific Northwest. And their raspy breathing.

Step away, girlfriend. You're playing with fire.

But she couldn't, wouldn't. The thrill swirling in her belly was whipping into a frenzy, reaching its hot tendrils out to the most intimate parts of her body. It had been so long, too long. Would there be any harm—

He broke eye contact first and dropped his arms to his sides, took a step backward. Gooseflesh raised on her arms, her skin nearly painful with the absence of his touch.

"You, ah, seem better now. I need to change." With no further preamble, he turned and walked down the long hallway that led to the bedrooms.

Wil didn't know whether to hoot or weep. His action had saved her from making a fool of herself, of totally breaking her professional code of ethics. It had only lasted for a nanosecond, but as they'd looked at one another, she'd actually contemplated bridging that six-inch gap between them and pressing her lips to his.

Correction. You wanted to stick your tongue down his throat. No, that wasn't true. Not completely. She'd wanted him to thrust his tongue into her mouth and trail it down her throat, her ribs…

Do. Not. Go. There.

Okay, so, yeah, she'd been swept up in the moment, from being in such close proximity to a practical stranger who happened to be in her target age range for dating. She could forgive herself for letting her hormones, which she'd obviously neglected for far too long, get the best of her. No harm, no foul, as her military colleagues would say. But what was unforgivable to her was that for several heartbeats, she'd completely forgotten the whole reason she was here, standing in the sorriest excuse for a kitchen. Heck, it was more bare-bones than most of the setups she'd experienced in the desert. In combat, no less.

Combat. Where a mistake like the one she'd just made could cost a life. Lives.

She ran her fingers through her hair, wrapped it up into a messy bun with the spare elastic ponytail band she always kept on her wrist. The best remedy for messing up was to not do it again. No problem there.

It had to have been that she was tired from a long day and a lot had been thrown at her in a short time. She'd be certain to get rest tonight, once she secured the house with the equipment CC used for each and every person, each location, they were assigned to protect.

As she went out to her car to retrieve the security equipment, the shock of cool mist on her cheeks snapped her out of her thoughts and made the almost-kiss seem a dream.

More like your worst nightmare. Compromising a client's safety would mean letting her family down. And it was something she'd never forgive herself for.

"I'll be right back—I'm going out to my car to get some gear. Stay in the house, do not even go on that nice deck until I return." She flashed him a grin—and hoped it didn't look like a grimace—before she went out the front door.

Toni answered Wil's call immediately.

"Please don't send me a text like that ever again, with only a tag to track and 'driver tried to kill us.' When it's a life-threatening situation, you call in to headquarters in that very moment, or as soon as possible afterward. Got it?"

"Yes, got it, but this—"

"No *but*s, Wil. This isn't the Corps. You'll find you have a lot more freedom in your work with CC, but not when it comes to someone trying to kill you. You're not on your own with any of this, ever." Toni's stern tone almost masked the thread of concern that thrummed through it.

"Got it." Wil knew better than to argue with Toni.

"The license tag number you texted came up empty. Are you sure you typed it in as you remembered?" Wil's stomach sank, and it wasn't from Toni's doubt as much as that it hadn't yielded any actionable information.

"Yes, I'm certain. My hands were still shaking from keeping us alive, but I made certain I copied it correctly."

"What about our client, Jay? What did he see?"

"Frankly, he was too busy reacting—tried to take the wheel over. Typical dude move." She was trying to convince herself more than Toni that that was all it had been. It had to have been pure reflex on Jay's part. The fact that he'd tried to maneuver them exactly as she had intended to was a coincidence, wasn't it? It didn't mean he had experience in advanced defensive driving skills, did it?

Doubt tickled her confidence.

"What aren't you telling me, Wil?" Toni must have heard the hesitation in her reply. Wil sighed.

"I don't know. And I mean that, really. He seems to…to know a lot more than he's saying. More than what I'd expect an accountant to know. He acted as if he knew exactly how to handle the situation, truth be told. And he definitely would have preferred to be the one driving."

"Of course he knows how to get out of a tight spot. He's working for the Clayton syndicate—they are the top dogs in this area and have the financials to put their thugs through whatever training they need."

"What kind of training?" Wil had never considered that criminals went through actual training. She'd assumed their experience was entirely on the job.

"Weapons, defensive driving, cybersecurity. But that's not my concern right now. Listen to what we found out." Wil remained silent as Toni went on to explain what the office had dug up on Veronica Clayton and Mack. "It's all smoke and mirrors, but at the end of the day I have to believe you're protecting the CPA for one of the largest criminal syndicates in the PNW. And there is a belief among the law enforcement invested in this that Veronica Clayton is about to try to pull off something big." Toni paused.

"What do you mean by *big*?" Wil asked.

"At best, she's trying to take over a couple smaller-scale syndicates, one in Seattle and one in Spokane. At worst, she's about to do a very hostile takeover of her most powerful rival, a syndicate with myriad resources."

"So it's like armed conflict, gangland style?"

"Conflict? More like war, Wil. Remember, these bad guys are armed to the teeth with the best money can buy. And they're never afraid to use their might."

Wil whistled. "So much for a boring security babysitting job. I'm glad my instincts about her were right, but I wouldn't wish this mess on anyone, especially CC."

"Veronica Clayton is unpredictable and power hungry, that's for sure. You're wading through very lethal water, Wil."

"So, do you need me to leave now?" Wil didn't see how, as a civilian, she'd be of any help with the syndicate. She certainly didn't want to protect a bad guy if she could help it. No matter how sexy his backside was.

"Not necessarily. I'd definitely pull you out if we were the only ones in on this." Toni paused. "The thing is, as you know, we work very closely with local law enforcement agencies, LEA. Federal, too, at times, although I don't have a bead on any feds working this at the moment. They've kept their involvement sealed up, for obvious reasons. I doubt that even Mom has any knowledge of the depth of federal involvement."

"Gotcha." Their mother had maintained close ties with her intelligence colleagues over the decades that she'd run CC—as much as possible, anyway. She'd also established a solid network of local law enforcement relationships by sharing useful CC intelligence with LEA whenever it was warranted. "You want me to stay on to get as much intel as I can, then? For the local LEA?"

"You catch on quick, sis. Yes. One of our…more official clients has asked for any help we can offer. Unofficially. We owe them for getting Jake out of a bind last year." She referred to their younger brother, who'd found himself in the crosshairs of an assassin last December. He ran CC's Portland office.

Excitement warred with trepidation as Wil processed this last bit. She yearned for an opportunity to prove herself in the field with her family, especially since the vast majority of her work for CC was going to be behind a desk working on cold cases. Protecting Jay was a one-off in-the-field experience for her. In the future, she'd be delegating fieldwork to her office subordinates. Her military training had underscored that one had to be a good follower to be a great leader. This was most likely her one chance to gain such detailed experience against a lethal foe.

The trepidation that had her insides quivering wasn't from fear of the danger this assignment all but promised. Nor was she afraid of Veronica or her thugs.

No, what triggered her reluctance was the thought of remaining in close proximity with a man whom she found herself attracted to more than anyone else she'd ever met.

"Willow?" Toni prompted.

"Sorry, lots of cogs turning. I'm still here."

"Look, if you have any hesitation, you don't have—"

"I'm all in."

She ignored her chaotic emotions, reminded herself that she was born to serve. First in the Corps and now for her family. Who knew how many families and innocents she might be able to prevent becoming victims if she could help bring down the Claytons?

Resolve cleared the cloud of confusion created by her inner conflict.

How hard could it be to ignore her hormones, anyway?

Jay splashed cold water on his face for the third time as he bent over the main bathroom sink. Carved from local mountain stone, the basin had the appearance of a natural pool in the oversize counter. How had she known he'd used the tub? He'd taken a cold plunge in this tub once, after he'd run ten miles on Saturday morning, and he'd thought he'd left it as pristine as when the contractors had finished. But she'd known. As he stared at the tub, his gaze landed on a very faint line on the side closest to him that he'd clearly missed.

Wil's astute observation was more confirmation to him that she worked for the Clayton syndicate, and reinforced that said crime network was watching him very closely. His gaze narrowed as he stared at the mirror, leaned in to inspect its edging. Were there tiny cameras in here? He hadn't detected any surveillance to date, but he might have missed it, especially if it was as high-tech as he knew Veronica's pockets could support. He couldn't risk bringing in equally high-tech equipment to check, either. If he got caught with it, they'd know he was a fed or assume he was from a rival syndicate. Either way, he'd be another one of Veronica's dead bodies.

Willow hadn't commented on how neat everything was in here. He'd have let her assume his geekiness extended to keeping his bed perfectly made, but even he knew that would be a stretch. The main bedroom boasted a four-poster king bed, and there had to be at least sixteen pillows arranged on it, ready for a photo shoot. He hadn't slept in here, ever. All the lights were on timers to mimic someone living in the house, and he had his own surveillance cameras set up all around the property. He'd be alerted at the first sign of an intruder while he was safely ensconced in his camper van, also equipped for bear—in the form of Clayton associates and any form of attack they could wage on him.

He had to be prepared for Veronica to send out more

henchmen at any point. She would never stop with the first
one she'd assigned to him, Willow O'Malley. Her professional skill had surprised him. First the car chase, and now
the way she'd handled clearing his space. Sure, he thought
her manner of sweeping the house had been for show, to
play the role she'd been assigned by Veronica. Act as a
bodyguard instead of giving away that she was Veronica's
early-warning detection for anything he did that was out
of line for a legit CPA. But. Doubt inexplicably tugged at
his assessment. For being a Clayton thug, Willow had put
on an awfully good show.

Maybe she really is ex-military.

She might be. But did it matter? Even if she was a former FBI agent, right now she was in the same boat as he
was, under the thumb of Veronica's whims.

He shook his head and refused to consider Willow was
anything but another hired gun. She'd follow orders to take
him out without compunction.

Best he remember he couldn't trust her, no matter how
much his lust for her hot bod urged otherwise. If only Veronica hadn't put Willow on his tail, he'd be free to make
the most of tonight, as he had the previous.

It had been quiet these first few weeks. So much so that
his only concern had been to stay low, keep his cover and
be prepared to call in backup to take down the Clayton
crime syndicate.

Until a wrench in the sexy shape of Willow had been
thrown into the mix. How could one person make such a
difference in so short a time?

He was furious with himself for almost losing it back
there in the kitchen. He hadn't been thinking, at least not
with his brain. For a split second he'd actually forgotten he
was undercover, and the heartbeat before that he'd pondered

letting her know that he wasn't who she thought he was. Insanity at best, a death wish at worst. Remorse washed over him and sat heavy on his chest. If he failed on this assignment, he'd be letting down his entire team. From the two agents awaiting the call for backup to the scores of intelligence agents trawling through years of forensic evidence to his superiors. It wasn't lost on him that many men before him had blown their cover over what they'd deemed hot sex. It was a plot known as a honey trap—the enemy would use a beautiful woman to lure agents to their doom by putting them in a compromising position they could be bribed over.

"Get it together." He softly spoke to himself, needing to hear the words as much as act on them.

He walked to the bureau and opened the top drawer, pulling out the single change of clothes he'd stashed in here, just in case. He'd expected the *just in case* to be when he was under attack, or when one of Veronica's no-necks knocked at the door. Something to give the impression that this was his actual home. He spied his backup pair of glasses and grabbed them. His eyes were killing him after pretending to care about what was on those blasted computer screens, staring through the fake, out-of-style frames. Since his contacts were disposable, he removed them and tossed them in the bathroom bin.

Jay shoved his limbs into a T-shirt, zippered sweatshirt and joggers he sorely wished were jeans. Thinking he'd switch into his favorite worn jeans once back in his camper, he took stock of the current situation.

Fact: Anyone hired by Veronica was on her side, and working for the bad guys. Period. If, on the sliver of a chance that Willow was a legit civilian security specialist, it made no difference as far as his protocol went. If he had to neutralize the threat she posed to his mission, he would.

He squared his shoulders and left the main bedroom for the kitchen, his game face back on.

Chapter 11

"Let me guess. You don't like Chinese takeout? Or is it that you don't do fast food?" Wil motioned at the food she'd put out on the tarp she'd spread across the living room floor.

Jay was getting on her last nerve. Since coming back inside after getting their dinner and talking to Toni, she'd had to pull teeth for any tiny bit of conversation. He clearly was still in shock from the news that his boss believed he was in enough danger to warrant a personal security guard.

Or maybe he's afraid you were going to jump him in the kitchen.

Which, in all fairness, wasn't untrue. She'd wanted to.

"Takeout is usually loaded with seed oils." He sniffed from where he stood next to one of the kitchen coolers. His frame seemed larger in the sweatshirt and joggers he'd changed into. They certainly fit him better than his ridiculous work clothes. His thighs filled out his bottoms as deliciously as his shoulders did his hoodie.

Stop. Right. There. Okay. She had to switch focus, memorize details.

She recognized a top-brand name tag on the bottom corner of his black hoodie. So the accountant was frugal with his work outfits, more extravagant with athletic attire. The image of his butt as she'd seen it this morning came to mind, and her internal flags raised, again. Something wasn't—

"I try to stick to olive oil, lard and butter. And I don't do refined carbs or dairy. Except for—"

"The butter. Got it. You know, Jay, I'm all about eating healthy, too, but desperate times call for desperate measures. Sometimes it's okay to chow down on what you might otherwise call junk food." To hell with manners. Client or no, she wasn't in the mood for a patronizing nutrition lecture.

He stared at her through his fashion-forward, thick-framed glasses, a far cry from the old-school glasses he'd worn in the office. Had he worn contacts earlier? Or did he have them on now, using this pair as a disguise? The old-school black frames didn't detract at all from his blue eyes, which were impossible to hide. Not that she'd have expected the studious man she'd met hours earlier to care about how his glasses affected his looks. Unless he wasn't who he said he was. She glanced at her phone, impatience making her forearms itch. Why hadn't Toni sent more information yet?

"Sorry this isn't up to your standards, but in my experience some days call for the most convenient solution. I should have asked for your food allergies or needs before I ordered, though." Point was that she was starved and there had been zero food in the house—and worse, no working stove for her to whip something up. When not pressed with work demands, Willow enjoyed putting together a meal. Cooking was her way to relax and unplug from whatever case she was on.

"I don't have any food allergies." He pushed off the wall and took a step forward. "Chinese is fine. I treat myself every now and then."

"Glad to hear it."

"I do prefer Thai, though." He sniffed.

"We can do pad Thai another time, then." Her stomach growled, and she didn't bother to apologize. She grabbed a small container of rice and the larger entrée container, a set of chopsticks, and three packets of soy sauce. With no place to sit, she eased herself down onto the cooler closest to her, grateful for its roomy top.

"There's kung pao chicken, sweet and sour shrimp with mixed veggies, and egg foo young. I didn't know what you'd like to drink, so help yourself to the beer or soda." As she spoke she watched him lower himself to his haunches, his back to her. Funny, he hadn't filled out his dress slacks as well as these athletic bottoms. She could just make out the elastic waistband on his underwear, which was a familiar eco-friendly, organic cotton brand—

"Ouch!" A sliver of chopstick lodged in between her thumb and forefinger as she rubbed them together. The brief discomfort was a small price for the most important reminder to keep her focus on her job, or at least on her dinner. Neither of which directly involved Jay's apparently firm, and obviously well exercised, gluteus maximus. Some runners lost their glutes; Jay was clearly not in that group. She'd always had a weakness for a man with a tight butt.

"You okay?" He scrutinized her with those damnably indigo eyes.

"Fine." She shoved a pile of sticky rice into her mouth to hide her discomfort.

He took his time piling rice and each of the entrées into one of the half-full containers she'd already helped herself to. To her surprise, he also picked up a pair of the disposable chopsticks before he sat across from her, using the cooler as a backrest. Without preamble he popped a sweet-and-sour shrimp into his mouth. She quickly forced her attention back on her kung pao.

This is all the spice you're getting tonight.

A good reminder.

Jay risked a quick glance at Willow. He hoped his nerd bit about seed oils had put her off enough that she'd leave him alone for the rest of the night. If he thought his time for contacting his FBI support team was limited already, it was made shorter by having to avoid her observation. He'd have to wait until she fell asleep—no bodyguard could stay awake for twenty-four hours—to make the trek through the woods to his van.

Maybe you're wrong about Willow.

Could Willow be legit, with zero ties to the Claytons? It did seem out of character for Veronica to have hired another woman, as she surrounded herself with a male-only staff. The intel he had on her supported the Claytons' usual modus operandi: Once they were finished with a contact or worker, they finished you. For good.

He ripped open three packets of soy sauce at once and doused his rice with it. Who ordered plain white rice with Chinese, anyway? If you're going to have it, why not go for lo mein noodles and fried rice, too?

His hackles rose and he looked up. Willow looked away, but not before he caught her wide-eyed hazel gaze focused on his hands.

"I'm hungry," he said.

"That was impressive. I had a hard enough time ripping apart one packet at a time." She moved her rice around with her chopsticks.

"I, uh, I've lived alone for so long I guess I've figured out how to get chow on the plate as fast as possible."

"'Chow'? Were you in the military, too?"

Uh-oh.

"Ah, no. I mean, yes. The reserves." Better to cover this mistake and any future ones with a white lie. Not unlike their military counterparts, FBI agents used a lot of similar jargon and nomenclature. Many special agents were military veterans. As careful as he was to maintain his undercover persona, a nonaccountant word slipped out here and there, especially when he was exhausted.

He wasn't tired physically as much as mentally. It was an emotional drain, playing the narrowly focused accounting nerd and hiding each and every piece of information he gleaned about Mack behind a vanilla, nondescript demeanor. He thought of earlier today, when he'd noticed there was a slightly larger crack between two pieces of the wainscoting in Veronica's office, right where it ran under her beverage sink. He'd wondered about a safe room for Mack's CEO and, more importantly, the most powerful mob boss second to only her Mexican cartel equals. And was pretty certain he'd found it. But he had to be cognizant of where his gaze was focused, as both Veronica and Derek were adept at reading expressions.

Added to the usual stress of undercover work was the weight of his suspicion that Veronica was getting ready to make a move to overtake one of the cartels. There weren't hard-and-fast red flags to signal an event was about to take place. Instead, Jay had to rely on his years of experience and his team's collective intelligence. Crime syndicates didn't make deals or merge as conventional businesses did. Each syndicate was an individual entity with its own personality.

Which contributed to his urgency to get Veronica in cuffs. She'd taken over the Clayton syndicate relatively recently—six months ago—compared to the years Jay had been analyzing Cal Clayton. Unlike Cal's forthright tendencies, Veronica was more slippery, an eel to Cal's shark. She liked to slither into rival criminal organizations, as she had with several smaller rings already. Veronica offered money and manpower to her target syndicates. Then, when it seemed all was running smoothly, she struck, sending scores of Clayton henchmen to seal the deal. It had been nothing less than a bloodbath in the last eight small organizations she'd successfully acquired. The other two main cartels in North America hadn't been happy with Veronica's moves, but hadn't made any efforts to stop her. Not yet.

Jay figured the cartels' head honchos let her get away with her game of kingpins because she kept paying them. It had been an intelligent tactic on Veronica's part. But even in the lucrative dirty business of drug and human trafficking, money had its limits. Veronica knew this, and her rivals knew it. By Jay's calculations, Veronica's tenure was at a tipping point. She needed to fish or cut bait.

Veronica Clayton never let anything go once Mack's fangs were sunk in. Jay thought of Mack Logging & Manufacturing interchangeably with Veronica Clayton's crime syndicate. He itched to get to his van, to send a report to headquarters. He tried unsuccessfully to not glare at the one obstruction keeping him from doing his job.

Their gazes clashed, and the increasingly familiar jolt of lust to his crotch was almost painful. Jay broke their nonverbal standoff. Willow's gaze was too dangerous a neighborhood for him to wander. Getting lost was inevitable.

"Branch?" she asked.

"Branch?" He was so used to playing the distracted nerd that he repeated her query without hesitation, costing him a second sharp look from her. "Oh, okay, I get what you're saying. I was in the Coast Guard."

"Really? That's a surprise. I mean, that you were in the military at all. Did you do financial stuff for the Coast Guard?"

"Yeah." *Phew.* Willow was unwittingly feeding him a decent backstory.

"Were you ever deployed?" she asked.

"Oh, no. My assignments for active duty were all Stateside, at a desk. You know, crunching numbers." He offered her what he hoped was a whimsical grin. *Whimsical.* Where had that come from?

It was impossible to tell how she took it, though, as she finished off her meal and stood. She nodded toward the back of the house, where the single working bathroom was. "If you don't mind, I need to shower and settle in for the night. Out here, of course. You can stay in your room, but I need you to follow some safety precautions."

"You've already installed the extra sliding glass lock, right? Isn't that enough?"

"The basic kit our company uses for all homes includes a lot more than sliding and French door locks. There are cipher locks and window locks as well. I think we're good for tonight, but you have to be ready to move, to get out of your room, at the slightest notice. Don't worry, I'll be right alongside you the entire time if that happens."

"Yeah, okay. So what's the protocol I have to follow?" Jay silently prayed his skepticism wasn't evident in his expression. If only Willow knew he wasn't a CPA…

"Keep your bedroom door open, and be prepared to take off through the sliding door if need be—I showed you how to unlock it. The window over your dresser is our backup egress—ah, exit point. Got it?" Clearly she wasn't leaving any room for him to misinterpret her request. Problem was, it felt so damn patronizing he wished he could let her know who he was and shut down her smug attitude.

Smug looked good on her, he hated to admit.

"Yeppers. Whatever you say. You're the security expert, Wil—ma'am." He studied her from behind his glasses. She sure did act as if she'd really been in the military, and recently. But would a hirable veteran work for someone like Veronica Clayton?

If they don't realize who Veronica really is they would.

"Right. Glad we're on the same page. I'll be done in a jiff. Especially since you only have cold water. And Jay?"

"Huh?"

"Come get me if you hear or see anything strange, okay?"

She didn't wait for his reply and walked away. Which gave Jay a perfect vantage point to observe the unmistakable feminine sway to her hips.

She's bad news, man.

Chapter 12

The press of Wil's shoulder blades against the bare floor in the living room woke her several times after she and Jay turned in. Her inflatable mattress pad's air pump had malfunctioned, leaving her sleeping bag as the only protection between her and the bare floor. She reminded herself that she'd had worse conditions during her brief combat stints, but thinking back, those had been few and far between. Because she'd been in a support role to the operational units, she'd usually slept on a real mattress or at least a solid cot.

She turned on her side and fluffed the extra sweatshirt she was using as a pillow.

Eeeeeeeeeeek.

Icy fear froze her to the floor, fighting the shudders trying to race down her back. It sounded like whatever had made the bloodcurdling cry was right here in Jay's living room. She lay next to the wall that separated the house from the woods that surrounded three corners of the structure. With the drywall gone, there was little buffer from the outside noises.

It's just a cat, or a skunk.

Quiet wrapped around her again, and she started to drift—

Yeeeeooooowwwww.

No. There it was again. Whatever animal it was, something had disturbed it. Wil didn't need to know exactly what kind of animal it was, but she had to make sure there wasn't an intruder who'd caused the animal's distress. She rose, albeit stiffly, and quickly slipped on the hiking vest she'd tricked out to carry every single tool she'd possibly need while working this case. After she'd zipped it, she slid into her favorite hiking boots. She'd never taken off the matching hoodie and joggers she'd slept in, knowing that her job relied on her being available at the drop of a dime—or an animal's cry.

Or bullet.

First things first.

She headed straight for Jay's room to make sure he was still safe. Annoyance rippled through when she came up against his shut door. She'd asked him to keep his door open, and she already knew he hadn't complied. She'd heard the door click shut right as she settled into her sleeping bag, but she'd let it go as all that really mattered was that Jay was securely in his room.

Now, with the chance of a threat outside Jay's bedroom door, she regretted not getting up and cracking his door.

Weapon drawn, she turned the knob slowly, silently. The door opened on a squeak and she held her arms out straight, weapon leading.

Cool air hit her cheeks, and she made out the white sheers that floated on a soft breeze. His outside door was open. There was no moonlight pouring in from outside, no visible night-light. She pulled a penlight from her vest pocket and quickly scanned the room. Jay's bed was flat, no sign he'd ever been in it.

What the actual—

Stay on task. She cleared the rest of the bedroom and

the main bathroom before returning to exit through the open sliding door. The security bar she'd installed for an extra layer of protection leaned against the wall adjacent to the door frame.

Jay had left of his own volition, then.

Maybe he's a smoker. Then why not smoke in the bathroom with its large window open? And she didn't smell tobacco, or any other kind of burning substance.

When she stepped onto the cedar deck, complete darkness enveloped her and she had to mentally envision the ten feet to its edge, as she'd measured earlier. She flicked on her penlight to make sure she didn't trip. Wil wasn't afraid of injuring herself as much as she was of making any more noise than she needed, and it bothered her no end that she had to use the penlight. Why hadn't she brought her night-vision goggles into the house? Instead they lay useless in the back of the company SUV.

It seemed hours, but according to her watch it took her less than three minutes to circle the outside of the house, passing through two tall cedar gates on either side and following the loosely graveled dirt path that connected them. Piles of paver stones lined the outside edge of the path, indicating that there was landscape renovation in progress. There was no evidence that anyone had so much as stepped on the damp earth, so maybe she'd simply heard those cries from a prey animal. Her SUV remained where she'd left it, in front of the garage, packed with construction materials. She knew her vehicle was the only transportation at the house, because she'd cleared the garage when she'd first arrived. Nothing was amiss.

Except for her missing charge, and his open bedroom door.

"You're kidding me, right? You lost our contract from his own home?"

She could hear Toni's accusation as clearly as if her sister was standing here next to her. Wil's imagination created a more strident Toni than reality, but not by much. It was a good reminder that she absolutely could not fail in this, her very first Cascade Confidential assignment in the field. Her only other in-person meeting had been with the missing girl's relative.

She silently swore and went back to the patio, trained the flashlight's beam on its edge and retraced what at dusk had seemed a simple straight line. This patio was a place to sit with a glass of wine after a long day of work and contemplate the stunning view, as well as the lush forest that rolled out to meet the horizon. Not to fear that an intruder had kidnapped her client. *Or worse.*

Willow gulped in the cool night air, forced herself to stay present, avoid the ugly thoughts that vied for her focus. When she again retraced the edge of the patio, something new stood out.

Stairs.

What she'd missed earlier were the steps that were almost impossible to see from the patio until one came right up to the edge where she stood now. The top step was carved out of the hillside and appeared to be no more than a railroad tie wedged into the rich earth. A railing that was out of sight of the house and patio began at the third step, and the stairs went down into what looked like complete nothingness. The stairway was incredibly steep but functional. Its steps were coated with the damp of night and fallen pine needles, with no noticeable footprints. Only a clawed animal's paw could penetrate what she estimated to be months if not years of coating. But as she shone her light to where it appeared the stairway ended, she saw what she needed. Footprints.

She had no choice but to take the steep steps.

Whoooooo.

It was her only warning before the dusty flapping of large wings moved the air in front of her face. Was that the brush of a feather on her head?

Her arms flailed as she startled, casting the light high, illuminating the silhouette of a great horned owl in flight. Majestic, even spiritually uplifting at any other time, but not when she was using every bit of self-control to stifle a scream. To her absolute horror, the flashlight slipped from her fingers and she helplessly watched it fly through the air before it plunged straight down. A soft *swish* told her it had landed far below, in the thick underbrush.

It doesn't matter. Keep going. You've got this. She had a spare flashlight—as in, her phone. Wil didn't need the extra light to get down the stairs, though. It wasn't worth the risk of providing a possible intruder with her location, and with not knowing how long this hunt would take, she had to conserve the battery. Wil gripped the slippery rail with bare hands and descended into the unknown. She took each step carefully, feeling with her toe for each next step's location before placing her weight down.

It wasn't more than thirty seconds by her GPS watch but felt much longer as she traversed the stairway without incident. Save for her having sweated through her clothing layers, and her labored breathing. Not from the physical exertion but from the adrenaline coursing through her every cell.

Once at the bottom, she used her phone light to see that there was a definite way into the ever-encroaching woods. Nothing fancy, but the flora was pushed down enough to recognize the path. She knelt down and more closely examined the ground. There were footprints in the damp grass, too.

Fresh prints.

Chapter 13

Wil loathed using her phone's light, but as she ventured farther into the woods, any ambient illumination from the house's back floodlights dimmed to near zero. If only she had the eyesight of the owl that had surprised her, this would be as simple as walking down a sidewalk. Why had she reacted to the owl as if she'd never been in a dangerous situation before?

Technically, she hadn't. Not as a civilian. And while the omnipresent weight of imminent catastrophic injury or death in a combat zone was the worst kind of stress imaginable, she'd at least been outfitted to deal with it. Plus she'd had a whole team to back her up.

Working for her family's security firm was fast becoming a lesson in the hard work her mother had invested into the business and her siblings had built upon.

Wil had to get a grip on the fact she wasn't in the Corps any longer, and had to accept that civilian life was just plain different. She kept in touch with her closest friends from active duty and each of them had struggled at times with leaving the old way behind and entering a more "normal" lifestyle.

Why had Wil expected her transition to civilian life would be any smoother?

Because I'm not starting a family, I have no one to worry about but me. She hadn't needed to find the perfect school district for her nonexistent kids—or make the choice to homeschool, as one of her friends with four kids had—and she certainly wasn't navigating an intimate relationship.

She mentally cursed herself for delving into her personal thoughts during an op. Staying silent was her top priority, as she didn't want whoever was in the woods to have any more warning than her footfalls, which she strived to keep quiet. Since she'd come back she hadn't even concerned herself with any inkling of dating, figuring it'd happen organically. Or with the help of a dating app, when she was ready. The only reason she entertained it now was because of one person.

Jay.

He was her assignment, and while physical attraction was always fun, *fun* didn't cut it at this point in her life. If she was going to get involved with someone, she'd go slow, make sure they were committed to the long haul.

She couldn't stop the snort she expelled. She wished she could tell her ovaries to slow down. The baby clock was ticking and she had never thought to freeze her eggs while on active duty. Mostly because she'd thought she and Chris were going to make it for the long haul—

Crunch. Distinct rustling to her three o'clock, followed by the unmistakable sound of breathing.

She froze, drew her weapon and lowered herself to her haunches.

And waited.

Jay threw back his third espresso and hit return on the keyboard, furthering his basic open-source search for Cascade Confidential and Willow O'Malley. He was expecting to find nothing, maybe several social media accounts for other women with the same name. It couldn't be his corporate babysitter's real name. He again reviewed why he had good reason to not believe Willow was a simple bodyguard. She had clearly been hired directly by Veronica Clayton. Veronica was wily and slick. She wasn't who she told her husband she was. According to their marriage announcement, she was "an experienced entrepreneur" and "responsible for several nationally recognized franchise operations" in the areas of "personal growth." With further digging, Veronica had turned out to be Belinda Barnes, an ex-con with a rap sheet that included forgery and drug dealing. Under two previous aliases, she had been married to elderly men who, while not in deep with a crime syndicate as was Cal Clayton, had both had deep pockets.

No, Veronica Clayton wasn't who anyone in the Clayton and Mack Industry circles thought she was.

Why would the henchman—er, henchperson—she'd hired as Jay's bodyguard be any different? As in, legit?

But from what he was finding in his cursory searches, Willow O'Malley was exactly the person she claimed to be.

"Well, color me too quick to jump to a conclusion," he murmured to himself in the small van, a habit he'd developed from long months on the road, moving in and out of his undercover roles. His display monitor revealed a simple yet apparently legitimate website for Cascade Confidential, with thorough descriptions of services offered and phone numbers for each of CC's satellite offices. He'd already sent what he knew about Willow to headquarters earlier this evening and was waiting to hear back from his partner.

His laptop pinged with an incoming request for a live video call, and he grinned. He and his partner often connected at an almost psychic level. It had saved their lives more than once. They'd started out together as rookies fifteen years ago and remained partners through several assignments and near misses. When their focus turned to organized crime in the Pacific Northwest a few years ago, Janice had recently married and desired to start a family. Meaning she wanted out of undercover work but was willing to stay on the team as an analyst. While he was undercover, Janice worked from the office back in Washington, DC, and lived with her family in Alexandria, Virginia. It was a good fit for all involved, and Jay was grateful the bureau had acquiesced to their request to continue working together.

The ping sounded a second time.

He clicked on the accept button.

"Hey, Janice. That was quick. Whatcha got?"

"Enough to say that Willow O'Malley is the real deal. She left the Marine Corps with an honorable discharge and retired at the twenty year point, much sooner than she needed to, based on her exemplary service. She had been promoted early no less than three times in her career, a very big deal in the Marine Corps. Someone who served with her revealed that she really left for family reasons, as in Cascade Confidential. It was founded by her parents, more specifically her mother, thirty-five years ago, when Toni, Aubrey and Willow were ages seven, five and three, respectively. The younger brothers, Kevin and Jake, who are thirty and twenty-eight, came along later. All five work for the family company. Their systems are locked down tight, I'd imagine, so unless we get a search warrant…"

He heard keyboard clicks and could see Janice squinting through the glasses she'd damned to all eternity the day they'd been prescribed.

"No need for a warrant. Not yet. In truth, you've validated what I've dug up, which is good."

"You can trust she's who she claims, Jay."

"I trust no one Veronica Clayton hired."

"Fair enough, but Willow O'Malley is an outsider to all of this. Veronica is keeping herself appearing legit by hiring from Cascade Confidential. It's a globally recognized brand when it comes to security of any kind."

"I'm not so familiar with them," he said.

"While I'm a bit surprised that there's something you don't know about where you're operating, I suppose I shouldn't be. You've had to be under the radar for so long, Jay. Trust me when I tell you that anyone in LEA in the PNW knows who CC is. They know her mother, who founded the company, Donna O'Malley, and the current CEO, Toni O'Malley." Janice went on to explain who Willow's mother was.

"Wait—I didn't know her as O'Malley," he stated.

"Right. But we all know who Domino is." Janice referred to a former CIA agent whose accomplishments in the field of undercover work were still studied by incoming agents in their basic school.

He whistled. "We sure do." His animosity toward Willow and her being a snag in his plans evaporated. Domino was legendary for her part in dismantling Russian syndicates in the last part of the twentieth century. The stunning part of her story was that she'd been still quite junior in the CIA when she'd accomplished all she had. She left undercover work behind and founded the now world-famous Cascade Confidential security company.

"So you'll be nice to O'Malley? She might indeed be the one to save your sorry ass, partner," Janice cajoled. She no doubt recognized the deflation of his ire by his tone.

Willow's still off-limits to you.

He checked the time on his computer and whistled again. "You're up awfully late, partner."

"More like early. Since the twins arrived, this is the only time I can get anything done. Be grateful I was able to handle this from home." Janice had twin boys who'd been born six months prior. The agency allowed her to work from home as much as feasible, while maintaining operational security by providing her with a secure laptop, router and comms unit.

"Trust me, I'm always grateful you're here, Janice."

Her sigh was audible. "I know. This has been a long op, Jay. Any idea how much longer?"

"Any day now." He couldn't promise anything and she knew it. Janice had as much intel as he did, maybe even more, when it came to the Clayton criminal syndicate and Veronica's anticipated takeover of at least two other known organizations. "This O'Malley security guard has thrown a bit of a wrench into my op plan, though. I won't be able to disappear as easily."

"Well, she's got a heck of a lot more to offer than a glorified mall cop would. Wait—isn't she on the property with you? How did you get past her tonight?"

"Fortunately for me, she decided to bunk down combat-style in her own sleeping bag in the living room. The main bedroom is down the hall and has its own French doors." He didn't mention that he'd cracked his bedroom door open enough to hear the distinct yet soft snores from Willow. And had been tempted to linger...

"I'm familiar with the house's layout. You know, blueprints?" She'd never had patience for his tendency to over-explain things, even less so since becoming a mom. He didn't blame her. Jay was sick of hearing himself talk about anything and everything. He certainly had to be overthinking every move he made here.

"Yeah, sorry 'bout that. I'm wound pretty tight." He stared at his empty espresso mug.

"You need a life after this, Jay. This isn't a way to live."

"Are you kidding me? People pay good money for my lifestyle."

"Living out of a camper van is one thing. But it's your escape and your work. The two should not be in the same space. I have to admit, though, that as extreme as it was to outrig it with the latest and greatest tech gear, it has paid off well for us and the bureau." She paused, and his hackles rose. Janice saw herself as his big sister. "Tell me something, Jay. Other than your work, what do you have?"

"C'mon, Janice. You're not being fair. Name one person on our team who's ever had a life outside of the bureau when they were undercover. Starting with you. Besides, you're seeing everything through mommy eyes now."

"Excuse me?" But she had already started laughing and he joined in. They were close enough and had worked enough cases together that they understood each other well. Janice knew that he respected her as much as any male counterpart and would never see parenthood as a detriment to any agent's capabilities.

"You may be right, Jay. It's totally fair to say my priorities have changed. But I don't plan on leaving my job, or our team. My undercover days are over, at least until these two dudes become grown men, but my passion for our mission remains. It's even stronger, truth be told. I want these little guys to have a safe world to grow into. Safer than it is with the likes of Veronica Clayton calling the shots."

"That's all our wish, Janice. For the record? You remain my first choice as partner for every assignment." Regret stirred in his gut. If Jay planned to stay in full-on operational mode, working undercover, he'd need a partner who would be willing to go into the field with him. He'd never trust anyone the way he did Janice.

He'd have to leave that worry for after he'd wiped the floor with Mack Logging & Manufacturing and the pernicious syndicate it fronted.

The unmistakable wail of an infant through his earbuds made him cringe.

"Now there's a set of lungs!" he exclaimed.

"No kidding. I gotta go. Stay safe, Jay."

"You know it." He disconnected. After a few quiet moments, he methodically began to shut down each of his systems. The van was battery operated while parked out in this small clearing amid acres of forest, using the solar panels installed on the roof, and an additional portable panel he left out if the day was predicted to be especially sunny. His tech equipment was designed to run with minimal juice, and he'd never run out of power yet.

Jay was another matter. His body ached from lack of proper rest, from the adrenaline that surged more often than not as he uncovered more and more insidious activities that Veronica's fingerprints were all over. But any thought of recharging himself had to be shelved. He had some bad guys to put away. For good.

Chapter 14

Her muscles started to complain, but Wil knew that whatever she had heard in the woods, it had been large enough that she'd hear it walk away. And like her, it had stayed still, with no further noise for the past seven minutes.

Unfortunately, the possibility that whatever she heard was human increased exponentially with each second. If it was an animal, it wouldn't be able nor willing to hide its breaths. Like her, whoever was out here didn't want to be detected.

She also knew not to assume it was Jay. If he'd been taken—which she didn't believe, based on how she'd not heard a struggle and there had been no evidence in his room or on the deck to support that—he could be anywhere.

Or already dead.

She shoved that thought into the compartment marked *don't go there*. Still, her heart pounded against her sternum and she had to consciously slow her breathing again.

Snap.

Then, footfalls. Not the four-legged kind. A slim figure stepped onto the path no more than six feet in front of Wil. She raised her weapon at the same time as the figure turned and ran down the path, back toward the house.

"Stop!" Wil yelled to no avail. Unwilling to lose the

shadowy figure, she bolted after it, silently willing herself to keep her focus on the person, who had to be dressed in all black or close enough, as she could barely see them. The only clue she had that the person was still in front of her was the sound of their feet crashing down as they fled.

At two points before they reached the stairs that led back to the patio, Wil thought she had them within her grasp. She'd reached out her hand to grab whatever fabric she could.

But her assailant was fast, and obviously better acquainted with the path. At least once they ran up the steps, the patio's motion-detector lights would yield information if not their identity.

But then they unexpectedly veered ninety degrees right and made a beeline for the tall cedar fencing that ran from the street to the woods. Wil followed suit and matched the person stride for stride, even clearing the six-foot fence no more than three seconds behind them. As she flew through the air—ready to roll onto her shoulders and back up in a move she'd done countless times on obstacle courses around the world—Wil tasted the thrill of nabbing this stalker. And finding out firsthand if they'd done anything to Jay.

If they had taken Jay, where was he now?

She rolled as she'd trained and snapped back to her feet, kept running. Until her foot landed a full six inches lower than the ground and caught.

"Oof." A jolt of pain stabbed through her ankle so sharply that her breath flew out of her as effectively as when she'd taken a steel I-beam to her ribs on an amphibious assault ship during an underway replenishment. Her chase was over. Finished.

Put a fork in me.

Her ankle screamed in protest as she got back to her feet,

fighting waves of nausea from the pain. As she straightened, she heard a car motor revving and she looked toward the street. She made out the fiery blinks of a large pickup's brake lights before it roared away, out of sight and away from her ability to do any more.

She leaned against the fence she may as well have stayed behind instead of vaulting. As she caught her breath, she struggled to figure out the next right action.

Jay.

Where was Jay? And was he still—

No. She wasn't going there. One motive pressed her to stand up, put weight on her ankle—the fact that she could told her it was a twist or sprain and not broken—and forge back to the path, follow it to its end. To wherever the assailant had come from.

She had to find Jay. Preferably alive.

The van grew silent as Jay went through the lockup procedures he'd done countless times since building and deploying the van. Janice and their immediate supervisor had at first raised their brows at Jay's idea to use the modified vehicle as his undercover headquarters, but once he'd proved to them and the bureau's techies that not only could he accomplish what he needed to in the field, but he could do it securely and under the guise of being another corporate or pandemic refugee who'd made the move to remote work, they'd applauded his ingenuity. 'Ingenuity' had been his boss's word choice. Jay knew he wasn't any smarter than his colleagues, but he had the advantage of being able to accept high risks with each assignment. He had no family to provide for, nothing to lose. Jay wasn't afraid to take risks, not as long as he brought criminals to justice and protected innocents from further harm.

He had a solid three hours of shut-eye ahead of him if he left the van now and slipped back into the main house. After one last glance into every nook and cranny of his portable office, he turned off all illumination and slid open the van's side door.

The moonless night offered no hint of light as he stepped down onto the carpet of cedar chips. The aromatic scent was sharp in his nostrils, not having dissipated in the last weeks since the property owner had acquiesced to having this very spot cleared of its trees. She'd indicated a desire to add on to her outside deck, so Jay had made certain none of the lumber went to waste. It was processed and awaiting her go-ahead at a local lumber yard—one that had nothing to do with Mack, which was rare in these parts. While Veronica seemed to be the big shark in the crime syndicate pool, Mack was one of several logging companies. Of course, it was the only one that had made millions laundering money, too.

He stood outside the van, ready to jump back in at the slightest warning, and switched on his red-filter flashlight. He'd considered using night-vision goggles out here more than once, but if the Clayton thugs saw him doing that, he was afraid it would cast suspicion on him being merely an accountant. How many CPAs carried night vision goggles, NVGs, for the hell of it?

He swung the beam around, making sure he was alone in the tiny clearing. His biggest concern until now had been the black bears, of which he'd seen a handful. They weren't interested in him as long as he made a lot of noise and didn't surprise them. As his days at Mack added up to a few months, and now Veronica had hired Willow, he knew the deal. The days of relative safety were numbered, if not over.

He gripped the slim flashlight with a new sense of urgency. He'd be a fool to think he'd be left totally alone for much longer.

He cast the scarlet beam over the surrounding trees, their trunks thick and gray, slowly turning as he inspected his surroundings, needing to ensure an undetected return to the house.

Without warning, a bright white light blinded him. One arm involuntarily raised to shield his eyes while the other hand wrapped around his weapon, a Glock M19. Not that he'd be able to use it with zero vision. Damn the bright light and double damn whoever was shining it in his face.

He cursed. NVGs would have taken care of him being night blind.

"Hey!" he yelled, squinting, as he tried to see past the harsh glare. "Identify yourself."

Silence.

Had Veronica's thugs found him?

Chapter 15

"Take your hand off your weapon, Jay. Go ahead and lower your flashlight while you're at it." She took a step closer to him.

"Willow? Why are you—"

"Is anyone else in that van?" Wil kept her voice steady; years of training had ingrained composure no matter the outside pressures or distractions. Which right now included the anger and frustration that had simmered her entire trek back along the wooded path, and her bum ankle. At least she could bear weight on it, so she assumed it wasn't more than a bad sprain. It hurt enough to force her to grit her teeth the last fifteen minutes of her hike, though, which only fueled her ire to the point where she wasn't sparing Jay an iota of patience. Client or no.

"I'm alone, Willow. Look, I can ex—"

"Just do what I tell you to. We don't have time for explanations." She watched him lower the pistol—a Glock, an M19, *interesting*—and shove it into his back waistband. Her brother Kevin carried the same weapon, but he'd been on a special SWAT team. What was a nerdy accountant doing with the same model?

Let it go. Jay was allowed to have his own protection. As long as he didn't aim it at her.

"Please tell me you know how to use that pistol properly," she said in an attempt to calm him.

He cleared his throat and it sounded almost like a laugh. Except he wouldn't be laughing unless it was something he did in response to being nervous, under stress. She had to assume he'd been stressed to be blinded. Bothered enough to pull his weapon on her, at any rate.

"Ah, yeah, I'm, uh, cool with the gun." The way he said *gun* didn't sound quite right. As if he was forcing his words. "It's kind of a hobby of mine. My brother and I go to the shooting range when we can. I, uh, like to hunt, too. Mostly rabbits, small stuff."

"With a pistol?" She couldn't help this last. Did he take her for a complete ignoramus?

"Of course not. We use crossbows when we're on a hunting trip. I'm trying to convey that I know my way around a, a gun." He pronounced *gun* as if it was a foreign word. "You don't have to worry about me accidentally firing it, or pointing it at you. Like you're doing with that flashlight."

She'd already been distracted tonight, first thrown off enough by her assessment that Jay would stay in his room, second that his remote location would be reasonably secure. She should have taken it for granted the earlier car chase was a harbinger of her more recent event of chasing off someone who'd probably been targeting Jay. Why else would anyone be in these woods, where Jay was?

A swell of warmth in her chest came on the heels of her involuntary sigh, both symptoms of her relief. *Jay is okay.* Finding her charge in one piece, alone and alive, was all that mattered.

She'd tromped through almost a mile of dark forest in the cold, damp night with her painful ankle, and had barely arrived at the clearing before she heard the van's door unlock. She'd had no idea who was in the van in truth. Sure, she'd assumed it was Jay and only Jay. But she had to be prepared for it to be anyone, maybe even one of the disgruntled employees Veronica had mentioned, with Jay as their hostage. Had two people taken him out here, with one returning to the house for an unknown reason, until they'd encountered Wil?

The long walk had given her time to review again what she'd witnessed and knew to be certain: There'd been no evidence of a struggle at the house. The sliding door had been left cracked open with a shoe in it, to prevent it from automatically locking Jay out. A kidnapper wouldn't have stopped to do that, in Wil's estimation.

Still, her gut had sunk with that line of thought. What if Jay *had* been taken? She'd never failed at a mission, and to have a civilian bodyguard situation go south was a nightmare. For Jay, for her family's agency, for Mack.

It wasn't with a little relief that she continued to aim the flashlight in his eyes, maintaining the upper hand.

"You always make it a habit of blinding your clients?" His verbal shot didn't delay him from complying, flicking off his light, shoving it in his pocket and holding both hands up in front of him. "Will you please turn the damn light off now?"

She aimed her beam at the ground between them, knowing it would take him several minutes to regain sufficient vision to make the walk back without her guiding him by holding his hand, or having him hang on to her shoulder.

Would that be so bad?

She brushed the thought away as she swiped at her forearm. The shivers were from the night air, definitely not lingering awareness from their almost-kiss. If she had more time to analyze her own emotions, she'd be frightened. Because the onerous events of today should have been more than enough to excise any lingering attraction she had toward the man.

A man who fit the bill for a CPA during banker's hours, but at breakfast in the diner and now tonight, outside his camper van, seemed to be another person entirely.

"Was someone out here with you, Jay? Tonight?"

He stilled. "No. Why do you ask?"

"Just wondering." She wasn't going to admit that she'd chased the interloper off his property. There was no way to know if it was his friend or her foe. Either way, they'd been a threat to her.

"What's going on, Willow? You seem really upset. What's happened?"

Damn.

She held up her hand in a stop gesture. "Hold on right there. Let me explain something again, Jay. I've been assigned to protect your—" she choked the words *sorry ass* back "—um, you, from the perceived threat environment at your place of employment. That means, according to the details spelled out in the contract, that I'm to know your exact whereabouts at all times. If you're going to leave an area we've agreed upon, let's say, your bedroom, not to mention your house, you are to let me know before you do so. You do nothing without me knowing about it. Am I clear?"

He shook his head as he slowly walked toward her, ignoring her command. For the life of her she couldn't muster the will to stop him. It was impossible to make out his expression as she kept the light angled away from both of their eyes. He stopped less than an arm's length in front of her, and she clicked off the flashlight to allow both of their eyes to adjust to the night, and to keep their location as hidden as possible. Darkness immediately surrounded them, the only illumination from the planets and stars, and a sharp-edged crescent moon. Dawn was minutes away.

"You haven't been out of the Marine Corps for very long, am I right?" The words slung low between them. His voice was deeper, with more of a command to it, then she'd noticed back in his tiny Mack cubicle. "Did you hear me, Wil?" His baritone rolled across the space between them, winding around her as tangibly as a warm blanket. Her pulse quickened, proving once again that Jay's nearness affected her. Distracted her. Kept her off her game. She had to dig deep to keep from drowning in the feelings this man triggered.

"Why do you think my military service or how long I've been a full-time civilian is any of your business?"

"You said that you're 'assigned' to protect me. Assignments are for the military or other…government entities. And in the military, especially the Corps, integrity is paramount. It explains why you'd think that what I do after work hours is any of your concern."

"It's all my concern if I can't protect you from a threat, Jay."

"My turn to disagree here, Wil. If you're really a civilian, working for hire, you've got one job to do. And that's to keep me alive. Plain and simple." At her silence, he persisted. "Don't worry, no one at Mack is going to find out that you lost track of me during your first eighteen hours on the clock. All I want in return is to be left alone."

"Are you threatening to report me?"

"And admit that I didn't play by Veronica's rules, either? No, it's not my first choice. But if you won't let me live my life the way I want to, off Mack's property, then yes, I may be persuaded to mention that your protection detail wasn't up to snuff."

"You were in the car with me when we were almost forced off the highway, right?" she reminded him. And remembered that he'd been awfully handy with the steering wheel himself. Just who was Jay? "You would have died out there if I hadn't been driving."

"Maybe. Or maybe they were after you."

She shook her head. "Nope." But doubt prickled her conscience. Was it possible someone was after her because of her work with Cascade Confidential?

It could be about the missing girls. The cold case.

"We're two adults, Willow. Let's agree to stay out of each other's business. You're welcome to remain at the house and give the appearance of protecting me 24-7. But when I'm off Mack's books, I'm on my own. I won't tell if you don't."

"Sorry, no can do, buddy." The reflexive quip shot out of her mouth, spurred by anger at his assumption that she had zero integrity. That he could bribe her with reporting her to Veronica, who would in turn tell Toni.

"I don't negotiate with clients." She bit her lip. Yes, she was no longer active duty, but combat missions with her team had made immediate, honest communication not only necessary but imperative. Lifesaving, in fact. Would he make the parallel—

"As in the US government doesn't negotiate with terrorists?" Incredulity punctuated his last query. Yep, he'd made the connection to her comparison. She'd all but said Jay was a terrorist.

The air stilled between them as the tension ratcheted. She stood rooted to the spot, deeply aware that she'd offended him, braced for his scathing reply.

A deep rumble sounded—from his chest. Before she could wonder why he was growling at her, Jay's laughter boomed. She wanted to resist its charm, resist him, but couldn't help how her shoulders relaxed and the tightness in her chest eased at the happy sound.

"Willow, in another time and place, you and I could make a good team." He wiped at his eyes.

"I'm so happy that I entertain you. And I do not agree. We are two very different people, Jay." She struggled to stay calm, to not run from what it was about him that put her on edge, made her want to flee and jump him at the same time. "And it's *Wil.*"

His laughter softened to a chuckle, and the air between them seemed…safer. Calmer, at least. She let out a long breath.

"You don't have to agree with me, Wil." Dang if her nickname didn't roll off his tongue as sexily as her given name. Maybe she should tell him to refer to her by her surname. Anything to keep a semblance of distance between them.

"Try to relax a bit here. You're on your first assignment since leaving the Corps, and you want to do good by your company. If you allow me to, I can help you do exactly that. But I'm only human, Wil. I've got to have some space of my own." He was good. Very good. Using her nickname as she'd asked him to, along with the convincing tone that made it too easy to look at him as more than a client.

She felt more than saw his arm raise, his hand stretch toward the van. "This is my home away from home. Where I go to read, chill, get out of the construction zone that's my house. You can give me this little bit of leeway, can't you? Look around us. Acres of woods, and I can attest there's no visible entry point from any major road." Which he didn't have to remind her consisted of one highway they'd almost been run off.

"Are you actually living in the van, then? By yourself?" As she spoke, a new explanation for the assailant hit her. Could it have been a woman? Someone he was involved with who'd thought she was the interloper? But why run away like that instead of calling for help from Jay?

"Most of the time I've lived out here, yes, to avoid the ugliness of the house renovation. I understand why you wanted me in the house, and I frankly didn't want to tell you about my van. No one at Mack knows that I'm pretty much a hermit," he continued, doubtless unable to read her disbelieving expression in the dark. "I was only here for a few hours, as it is."

"Uh-huh. You could have told me you wanted to be here for only 'a few hours.' I have no problem bunking out here." Wil realized that she was inviting herself into a very small, compact camper van. She'd seen many on the road with her Jeep, had a friend or two who'd taken to the roads after their military stints and lived exclusively out of them. The last thing she wanted was for Jay to think she wanted to be anything more than his bodyguard. "I can sit out here while you're inside. I'll need to regularly patrol the perimeter of the property either way, which would give you your space. Looks to me as though you have a lot of options, Jay."

"No. That won't work. I'm possessive of my private space. There's not a lot of room in there, to be fair. You know, after having to work all day with all the people at Mack. I'm used to working remotely, especially since the pandemic shutdown." She gritted her teeth at the nerdy inflection that had crept back into his tone with the weak explanation.

Jay the CPA was back. And she didn't believe any longer that the accountant was the real Jay, the man she'd briefly encountered in the diner, the man she'd caught leaving his camper van minutes ago.

His sigh was overly dramatic to her ears, especially from a man who was the epitome of boring while working as Mack's CPA. "If you don't mind, I really need to get some shut-eye before work. Veronica wants several spreadsheet reports presented to her before nine o'clock, so I have to be at my desk by seven. That leaves me two hours of power napping." He paused. "I don't suppose you're going to let me sleep out here?"

"No. Not if you don't want me in there, not tonight." She couldn't risk that the assailant she'd chased wasn't looking for Jay, or that they were the same person who'd tried to run them off the road. "Staying out here is too risky after our road adventure. There's no protection other than the thin walls of your camper van, plus we'd be sitting ducks until I have a chance to clear the woods in the daylight. The house is our best bet for the rest of the night."

"Whatever. Nothing I'm going to say will change your mind, it seems," he said.

"You're right about that. Before we head back, though, tell me something, Jay. How long have you put on this nerd act? Is it just for the benefit of Veronica and Derek, something you had to do to win the Mack position? Or is it something you have to do to survive in the CPA world? I'm not being facetious here, either. I truly don't know much about the world of finance."

She waited, sensing the hesitation in his stillness, his lack of a quick comeback.

His sigh was short and full of resignation. "I'm too tired to process what you're asking me, Wil. Finance and accounting are actually two very separate functions in a corporation. Look, it's been a long night. I admit that I should have told you I was coming out to look at the stars. I promise I'll stay in my room, in the house, until we leave for Mack in the morning. Now, can we get back so that we can both get some sleep?"

"Right." She motioned with her light toward the woods. He knew the way here better than she did and could get them back without the beacon alerting any interlopers. "After you."

Jay didn't reply as he stepped out and led them into the forest.

If she'd had a sliver of hope that he was going to offer insight into his apparent double personality, it was crushed with each step they took in silence back to the house.

Chapter 16

Jay made sure he stayed true to his promise the next morning, not emerging from his room until he was showered, dressed and ready for the drive to Mack. He caught himself about to turn the bedroom's door handle for a second time and pulled his hand back. He was so used to going into the kitchen and making himself a cup of instant coffee. He loathed the pseudobrew, but with only two hours of sleep, caffeine in any form worked for him. Best he wait until they were on the way in to Mack. Surely Willow would stop for coffee and a takeaway breakfast? Problem was, he was looking more forward to having another meal with her than reporting to work.

Crap.

He was so close to wrapping this case yet had never felt so far away from the finish line, thanks to Willow standing in his way. After two full years of prep to get here— including fooling Veronica Clayton and her henchmen, as well as an intermediary syndicate, into believing that he was to be trusted—he was at the behest of a spanking-new security agent. She was good, he had to give Willow that. She hadn't fallen for his shtick that he was simply a numbers guy with no interest in or knowledge of the actual operations that paid the bills. Willow O'Malley put the likes of Veronica and Derek to shame.

Sure, Veronica and Derek had to suspect by now that he was aware of their money laundering, at least at some level. But he'd never given them an iota of evidence that all he concerned himself with were the numbers he reported daily to Veronica, and of course several times throughout the workday as requested.

If he wasn't so anxious to get to the crux of Veronica's criminality, to gather all evidence and arrest her, he'd be able to think more about how stunning Willow's intelligence had proven over the very short time they'd been forced to work together. Okay, maybe not together, but side by side. She'd unknowingly walked into a high-priority FBI operation where they'd placed one of their top undercover agents. He wasn't being self-aggrandizing to recognize his value to the agency, to justice. Yet Willow had wasted no time in slicing and dicing his disguise, suspicious of him after only observing him for half of a workday. Running into one another in the diner hadn't helped his incognito efforts with her.

"Let's get some chow." She didn't give him a choice as she pulled through one of the ubiquitous drive-by coffee stands that heavily sprinkled Washington State. "What do you want? Breakfast sandwich?"

"Yeah, and a double-shot red-eye." He needed the extra energy boost from the espresso added to the regular black drip. She repeated his order to the barista who leaned out of the tiny store's window and ordered an extra-large oat milk latte for herself along with their food. The tiny town Jay lived in wasn't that far from Spokane, and it allowed for the same access to high-quality coffee as the Seattle-Tacoma area. Except the prices were markedly lower and the brew just as good if not better. The juniper-scented air wafted through her open window, blending with the strong coffee aroma.

"Here." He handed her his phone. "Use my card to tap."

She offered him no more than an impatient wave.

"It's a write-off for Cascade Confidential." She tapped her own phone onto the point-of-sale device, then accepted their meal from the barista.

"Thank you." Willow placed the steaming-hot cups into the beverage holders in the center console and tossed the bag of sandwiches at him.

"Hey, watch it. I don't want to get sausage grease on my suit." But he'd caught the bag no problem, and waited for her to park before handing her a napkin and her half of the meal.

Willow didn't utter another word until she'd wolfed down her breakfast. She wiped her mouth and hands, then sank into the leather seat, holding her latte as if it were the Holy Grail. He couldn't tear his gaze from her lips as she took her first sips of coffee.

"Mmm. That's what Mommy needed." Her expression was of sheer bliss as a shock of awareness hit Jay's gut. And went further south.

"Mommy? Do you have kids?" He'd never thought to ask her if she was single or in a relationship. He'd assumed she wasn't. It wasn't like him to ever assume anything. Belatedly he remembered Janice's comments on Willow last night. Janice would have mentioned a family, children. His gut sank at the confirmation that Willow was the exact distraction he didn't need.

Too late.

She laughed. "No, no kids, and no partner, either. 'What Mommy wants' is an expression our parents always used, and now we use it with my sister Toni, who has a daughter. It's kind of a family inside joke."

"I thought you were single, since you never mentioned a family other than your siblings." He couldn't explain why he had the urge to defend his assumption with her. Why did he care about someone he'd only just met? And would never work with again?

This would be easier if he didn't know that Willow was the real deal. She'd been a devoted Marine and now was applying the same dedication to her position in the family business.

They sat in comfortable silence, and he wished he'd ordered two of the hearty sandwiches.

"What about you, Jay? Single and no kids, too?" Willow's query almost made him laugh. She wasn't one to ever let an opportunity to dig into his life escape her.

"Guilty as charged. What made you think that?"

"I don't know a lot of folks who live like you do and have a family, too." She looked at him, and he swore the gold flecks in her eyes were actually twinkling. "Unless there're gnomes out in that forest?"

He chuckled. "No, no gnomes."

When she glanced away, his entire body felt cooler, as if the sun had set in the desert. They both looked through the windshield as they enjoyed their caffeine fix. The morning light fell in golden shafts through the tall cedars, and leaves drifted lazily from an oak tree's thick boughs at the edge of the parking lot, sprinkling leaves across the gravel. The peace of the scene sharply contrasted with the constant whir of his mind, always anticipating the bad guys' next move, always trying to stay several steps ahead. And now, fighting the increasing pull of the woman beside him.

"You never answered my question last night." She didn't

look at him, but her words pinned him as effectively as her hazel gaze would have. So she hadn't forgotten that he'd blown off giving her a reason for how he dressed and acted at Mack. *Damn.*

He measured his words before he spoke, sensing that the jig was going to be up with Willow if he wasn't very, very careful.

"I was tired, and it was late. And you're right, I do play more of a nerd than I need to at work. I am used to working in environments where if I'm doing my job well, I blend into the background. But if I mess up, an entire corporation can go under. So I do my best to not stick out at all."

Silence. Was she buying his lies?

"Well, whatever you have to do, Jay, I'd appreciate it if you keep it in mind that I have a similar role here. We keep you alive and safe through whatever *expansion* Veronica was talking about yesterday, then Cascade Confidential gets another feather in its cap and future business from Mack and similar companies. But if anything happens to you, it doesn't just mean that I dropped the ball, or that I'll lose my job. It means a hit to my family's business and the legacy my mother began when she founded CC."

Willow wasn't saying anything he wasn't already aware of, but he held back from letting her know he'd vetted her. To be fair, until last night he would have said he didn't care about her family business's fate. He'd worked, clawed, dug and survived undercover for too long—his entire team had sacrificed countless days, months and myriad holidays away from family—to afford him an ounce of empathy for Willow or her position. But now that he knew she was legit, and not part of the Clayton crime ring, he couldn't help but care.

The fact that you're attracted to her doesn't hurt.

"Got it. Can we agree that we need to have each other's back enough to get through the next few days?" *Shoot.* He shouldn't be referring to any kind of timeline. She'd already figured out he was putting on a front; it wouldn't take her much longer to discern he was LE.

"You think the merger, or acquisition, or whatever civilians call it, will be over by then?" she asked. "Veronica made it sound as if it wouldn't be long, and my contract isn't supposed to go much past this weekend."

His insides relaxed. Her question sounded like genuine curiosity and not suspicion.

"I do." He knew he sounded more assured than he was. But it was because he hoped to have Veronica and her organization in cuffs as soon as humanly possible.

Her phone screen lit up and she raised it to check her texts. The morning light reflected around her face in a halo of illumination, accentuating her beautiful features. Her full lips pursed as she read a text or email. The sexual tension he'd been able to ignore this morning shot through him, and he forced his gaze away from her before he leaned in and kissed her, hard.

Instead, looking away and focusing on the morning sky had to suffice. Anything to take his mind off Willow.

Back at Mack, Wil's phone vibrated silently and Toni's name displayed on its screen. Toni had been trying to reach her since the drive in, but she hadn't wanted to take a call in front of Jay. Wil welcomed the distraction from being bored out of her mind in Jay's workspace. It was almost noon, so she had a good excuse to get out of the building for a short while.

She peered over the cubicle walls and determined many of the other employees working this weekend had left, for lunch or perhaps home. She sent the call to voicemail and fired off a text to Toni.

Give me a sec.

She stood and stretched, using the motion to inspect the office. Yeah, the place was pretty much emptied out, as she'd expect it to be. It was a Saturday in September, one of the prettiest seasons in the PNW. There had never been more than half the employee force present since this morning, when she and Jay arrived right on time, a whopping four hours of sleep between the two of them.

They'd spoken minimally since last night, having traversed the path back through the woods in silence, with brief *good night*s before she had returned to her spot near the front door and in full view of Jay's bedroom door. He'd acquiesced to keeping his door open, and she'd vowed to herself to not be duped by him again. When he'd gone into the bathroom, she'd installed a tiny but mighty motion detector on the edge of the sliding door frame. She'd be alerted if one of the sheer curtains moved, and certainly if Jay attempted to leave again.

But there'd been no further drama last night, and only a brief verbal spar in the kitchen this morning when she'd discovered there was only one packet of instant coffee left. She'd made a silent vow to never drink the stuff again after she'd lived on it whenever she'd been stationed downrange. The lack of any real coffee, or much of anything else in the nonexistent kitchen, was proof that Jay was used to making coffee in his camper. Hence, he'd never lived in the house, something she should have picked up on immediately when she'd secured the place. Cascade Confidential was a security firm, and her sister had sent her to some high-cost training that wasn't meant to be ignored just because Wil had thought this assignment was glorified babysitting. And she'd cleared the house after the attempted car crash.

If she wasn't careful, resentment was going to take root over her anger at herself for being fooled by Jay in the first place. Which was plain silly, as she barely knew Jay. And yet, it seemed as if he'd always been in her life.

If this was what living in the civilian world meant— getting too close too soon to a sexy stranger—maybe she'd made a big mistake in leaving the Corps.

And now Jay had admitted that he basically lived in the van and used his job as an excuse for being such a dweeb at work. If only she could accept his explanation at face value, not look for the meaning behind his every word. For some reason his story didn't all add up as legit, though. He wasn't who he professed to be, she was certain of it.

Her morning latte and breakfast long gone, her stomach growled for lunch. Jay didn't seem to notice as he remained at his desk, his focus glued to the computer screens. Time to give in to her restlessness. And she needed privacy to have her conversation with Toni.

"Hey, Jay, I'm going for a quick walk around the parking lot. Please stay here until I get back." She grabbed her small backpack from where she'd placed it earlier, under his desk.

"Is that an order, Wil?" Soft yet no less demanding. The Jay she'd glimpsed at his home hadn't totally disappeared behind his geek CPA persona.

She stood but kept her gaze on him until he looked away from the screen. She'd guarded herself against his annoyance but the sensual heat that turned his blue eyes aqua sent a shock of awareness straight through to her personal parts. Wil swallowed and forced herself to hold his gaze despite the logical part of her brain that warned her to take a step back. But words wouldn't come.

"Well?" he prompted. His voice remained low, and she willed her gaze away to quickly scan the rest of the bullpen. No sign of Derek, and the few remaining workers were several cubicles over.

Two can play at your game, Jay.

"Well, what?" She involuntarily licked her lips.

Danger, girlfriend. Stop. It. Right. Now.

Too late. This chemistry between them was unlike anything she'd ever felt before. Lust, definitely. Maybe even what some might refer to as love at first sight.

Too far.

Was this a pull of attraction so strong that she was ready to abandon her responsibilities to keep Jay alive and Cascade Confidential's impeccable record intact? No. No matter that her fingers itched to take her clothes off. She slowly shook her head.

"Are you giving me an order or a suggestion to stay right here?" Jay spoke before she could come up with a sane response. The corners of his lips tugged upward in what had to be amusement. It wasn't at her expense, though. She didn't know Jay well, had known him for less than thirty-six hours at this point. What she did know about him was that the vibe coming off him right now was new. As if he was okay with her looking past his faux-nerd layer. At the sharper, more honed edge she'd glimpsed last night outside his camper, and before that, at the diner. Why now?

She had to keep her cool. *Jay is not trustworthy.* That's what Toni had told her, anyhow. She hated that her instincts were telling her the exact opposite, and it wasn't only her sexual desire. There was something deeper going on here that she couldn't identify.

She leaned back and looked away before facing him again. Technically, Veronica Clayton was her employer for this contract, but the CEO had made it clear that Wil was on her own unless a problem arose. Meaning, a problem had better not arise, because it would mean Jay was either injured or worse. No longer active duty, she needed to learn how to play by civilian rules while still getting her job done.

"It's officially a request, but for both our sakes, consider it an order." She walked away before he could reply.

Chapter 17

Willow's bottom was all Jay wanted to pay attention to as she walked away, not that he needed to verify she was the most attractive woman he remembered ever meeting. He'd checked her out earlier this morning before he'd had a chance to stop himself. She wore formfitting black business slacks that emphasized her curvy assets. The white button-down blouse that he'd only caught glimpses of under her brown leather jacket had acted like a signal. Because Willow had left that third and critical button unbuttoned, allowing torturous hints at what he now knew was a pair of generous breasts. He'd made out their shape in the kitchen last night, when Willow had first emerged from the shower in only a T-shirt and athletic joggers.

He shouldn't have goaded her just now. He was playing with fire.

Goaded? More like flirting, and beyond. It was so easy—too easy—to let the need that stormed his insides come out in front of Willow, now that he knew she was legit. Willow could actually be an asset to his op.

He could trust her with the truth if he wanted to.

No. *Never.* He'd never brought an innocent civilian into an undercover op, and he wasn't starting now. Not with the deadliest crime syndicates he'd ever studied about to go to war. Sure, Willow had served in the Marine Corps, which made him respect her, plain and simple. But wearing a uniform wasn't the same as taking down established cartels and slimeball crooks.

Or was it?

He sighed, forced his attention back to the firm's numbers. Their fake numbers, from all he'd analyzed last night in the camper and corroborated this morning.

Derek's foot hit the cubicle wall a second before he spoke, shaking the entire unit. "Where's your rent-a-cop, J-man?"

Jay's jaw clenched against the biting retort he'd love to lob at the clod who leaned over the fabric wall, his nose no more than twelve inches away from him, his beady eyes bouncing around the numbers on the computer display.

As if he knows anything about finances.

"I don't know where she is," he lied. "She said she's taking a break." As he spoke, Derek maneuvered himself around the wall and stood next to Jay in the cubicle.

"Is that right? Not very protective of her," Derek said.

"I imagine she's not so concerned when Mack has so much of its own security." He didn't bother to look over his shoulder. That would put him at eye level with Derek's gut, which the dude prided himself on "working into a six-pack." Jay knew it had been Derek's way of putting Jay in his place as a "number cruncher," which was fine with Jay. It meant that he was doing his job well enough to maintain an undercover role. Derek had obviously fallen for his non-athletic demeanor and accepted Jay as no more than an office drone, as a syndicate lackey not unlike himself. Jay bit the inside of his cheek to keep from smirking.

"She's supposed to be keeping you safe. How's she doing

that if she's not right here?" Derek's feigned indignation grated.

"You'd have to ask her, buddy." He knew his quip wasn't in line with a nerd, but so be it. Let Derek think—

"I'm not your buddy, pal. You work for me."

"Of course." *You sad sack...* Nope. He'd save the verbal assault for when he saw Derek in cuffs.

"I can't talk when I'm inside the Mack building, not even in the restroom. I'd be surprised if Veronica Clayton doesn't have the entire place bugged. The employees all act as if someone's always looking over their shoulders. I have to make this quick." Wil summarized last night for Toni, making sure her sister knew she was up to the task of protecting Jay but wanted to know who the heck he really was.

"What have you found out?" As she spoke, Wil eyed a hulky security guard through the windshield as she sat in the SUV. He sat at his station, just inside the building's main employees' entrance.

"Before I give you the lowdown on Mack Industries and the Clayton family in particular, I want to apologize for sending you in there unprepared. This isn't the way we usually operate." Toni's unexpected apology raised Wil's nape hairs, and she involuntarily shivered. Were her suspicions about Jay correct?

"That doesn't sound good, sis. Spit it out."

Toni's sigh said more than her explanation ever could. "Well, let's just say if Mom knew I'd sent you out on this job without doing my due diligence, or at least having Denice—the librarian—do the background check, she'd fire me and be back in this office in a heartbeat. There would be no questions, no regrets on her part. I've broken the cardinal Cascade Confidential rule—always know your client."

"You've been busy. We all have been swamped, as you said. And what's stopped me from looking into Mack and the Claytons sooner, if we're honest?" Maybe if she emphasized that they were a team and background checks were the responsibility of their whole team, not just Toni, her older sis would let go of some of the burden.

"Don't patronize me, Willow. You wouldn't have found a whole lot without access to our private files on the PNW syndicate that CC has had on-again, off-again brushes with. Only LE and us have this information. It's not available to the public, and won't be, until the bad guys are brought down."

"I would have only needed to log into the main server." Willow said.

"None of this is on a server—it's all hard copy, in our vault."

"You got my attention with 'PNW syndicate' and 'hard copy.' Talk." Her patience was kaput.

"The PNW Syndicate, known as Badger by LE, has been in the news here and there, but not a lot, as in, no formal charges have been filed by any law enforcement. I know that at the very least each county sheriff in Washington and Oregon has been feeding information to higher-level state and federal authorities. The feds took over running the counter–crime syndicate operations two years ago, from what I'm looking at, due to Badger's increasing interstate and international operations with a Mexican cartel. It appears that there's about to be some kind of showdown among these bad players, sis." Toni wasn't holding anything back.

"How are Mack and the Claytons tied in with Badger?" Willow asked.

"More like how they *aren't* tied in. There has been a

long-standing concern and not a few allegations from the
local LEs of money laundering. The lifestyle enjoyed by
Veronica Clayton and her husband—before he became an
invalid—far exceed what even the most lucrative logging
companies could ever support. And there's the issue of all
the possible business fronts that have popped up in Pine
Hills since Veronica took over as CEO."

As Toni read aloud the list of a dozen businesses, Wil
used her phone to look at a GPS map of Pine Hills, con-
firming where each business was located.

"Gee whiz, that's everything from the Creperie restaurant I overheard some employees discussing at the break
counter to the spa and a hookah lounge." Wil looked back
through her windshield to find the security guard had chosen this moment to take a stroll outside. He turned to start
walking down the aisle of cars where she'd parked. She
switched her phone from the car speakers and held the
phone to her ear, not willing to risk the guard overhearing
any part of their conversation.

"It's typical of the Badger syndicate the Claytons seem
to be synonymous with."

"So maybe the merger that Veronica mentioned is actually a syndicate takeover. Badger's going to absorb the
Mexican cartel." She thought aloud, not expecting Toni
to reply. "Well, we've only been asked to protect Mack's
CPA. A small job in light of all of this. And one we can
pull out of ASAP. We don't want Cascade Confidential anywhere near this, right?" But even as she asked the obvious
question, as much as Toni's new information had validated
Wil's suspicions, something deep inside Wil didn't want
to let go of the fantasy that Jay was a good guy. Not one of
them—Badger or otherwise. She opened her mouth to tell
Toni her instincts—

"Sis, you've got to assume that Jay is not an innocent or employee of Mack. He's another criminal working for them. A Badger." Toni crushed her thoughts before she articulated them.

"Gotcha. I do. But you haven't told me to leave." Wil hoped Toni was overreacting, but in her gut she knew that somehow she was in deep here.

"No, I haven't. Listen. I called in a favor to one of Mom's connections." Toni didn't elaborate and didn't have to. Donna O'Malley's connections ran the gamut from her former employer, the CIA, to all federal law enforcement agencies and the many tiers of state and local jurisdictions that existed in the PNW. Donna had put Cascade Confidential on the map because of her tireless efforts in networking and proving time and again that CC was an operation that could be trusted.

"Go on," Wil said.

"Veronica Clayton requested five days of protection from us, claiming the perceived threat is from former employees, maybe a few environmental protesters. But from what Mom's contact told me, the federal agencies watching Badger believe that the syndicate is totally under the purview of the Claytons. Mack Logging & Manufacturing, aka Badger, is vying to acquire three major industries within the next days if not hours." Toni named three Fortune 500 companies, one each in Washington, Oregon and Idaho. "It just so happens that these three industries are the bread and butter—for money laundering—of the Mexican cartel. If Veronica Clayton is capable of pulling this off—and all sources I've been able to tap agree she is—it will make her the top kingpin for the entirety of North America."

All thoughts of eating lunch dissolved into Wil's churning gut. She'd always relied on her gut instincts, and this was proof she couldn't.

"You sure sound convinced, Toni, and I believe you. But it doesn't put me personally in a bind, and I'll be able to protect J—my client. Except…" She worried her lower lip with her upper teeth. "I don't know. It's probably nothing. Remember, I'm trained in cyberwarfare and more physical types of problems. I'm not an intelligence analyst or caseworker by a long shot."

"But your impressions are no less valid. What were you going to say?" Toni's self-recrimination was gone, replaced by her usual no-nonsense demeanor. A bit of the tension over all of the heavy information dump eased and Wil rubbed the back of her neck, noting the security guard was at most fifteen seconds from passing her SUV. Too close for comfort, close enough to observe she wasn't eating lunch but on the phone.

"Look, I can't talk much longer, but last night I found out that my client isn't actually living in the house he reported he owns. He's staying out in the woods, almost a mile from the building, in a camper van."

"We can't think he's not one of them, Willow. And you know what that means."

"That I'm protecting the man she needs the most, because funding her illicit activities is the top goal here?"

"No. Veronica Clayton hired you to take fire from the syndicates she's trying to overtake. You're nothing to her but a Kevlar vest for her CPA. And he's not someone you can trust, either. How do we know he's really a CPA? He's probably doing more than accounting. My guess is that at best, he's a longtime syndicate member working for Veronica. At worst, he's a mole sent in from the Mexican syndicate, who will help identify the exact time for her to make her move. Either way, he's on the wrong side." She didn't need to say what Wil already had figured out: Jay wasn't on their side.

"He, he doesn't seem like he's a bad guy, though." Her voice wavered and she damned her attraction to Jay to the pits of Hades.

"They never do." Toni's reply was quick, no-nonsense.

"But…" Wil didn't usually share the intimate relationship details of her life with Toni. The emotional tolls of her relationships, sure. But this was different. She owed Toni an explanation as to her hesitation over judging Jay as one hundred percent criminal. She'd almost kissed him. Would her body betray her, allow her to be physically attracted to someone who should have been firing off her internal alarms? She'd had no such instinct with Jay. Only…desire.

"But what?" At her silence, Toni exclaimed a high-pitched swear word. "Oh jeez, Willow, please tell me you don't have the hots for this number cruncher." Toni's attempt to break the silence and lift the mood was ill spent. Guilt sent heat to Wil's cheeks.

"Please. He's as geeky-looking as you'd expect, and not much of a conversationalist. It's hard to imagine he's a thug." Except for how he filled out his clothes when he wasn't wearing an oversize suit, how he'd walked so assuredly out of the van before realizing she was watching him.

"But you said he admitted the nerd profile is just that, a false front? And you still find him hot." Toni laughed. "Sorry. I'm not making fun of you. I'm actually relieved that you're human. Look, don't beat yourself up about this. I know you're a consummate pro and the thought of even admitting that you might have an inappropriate crush is anathema to you. But this isn't the Marine Corps, Wil."

"But I'm still me and I have my own code of conduct."

"Easy, sis. Nobody's going to court martial you for finding a client sexy. But they could file a sexual harassment charge if you try to act on it, if it's not mutual. Either way, stay away from him, Wil. It's your safety at stake here as far as I'm concerned."

Had it been mutual? Or had she mistaken Jay's body language, the smolder in his irises?

"You sound as though you have some experience in that regard." She tried to keep the frosty tone out of her voice, but honestly, Toni was annoying her. She felt bad enough for her almost-transgression last night. Now, knowing what Toni had found out, she had all the more reason to keep her distance from Jay. Her aggravation was with herself, not her sister.

"I…do." Toni's soft reply tugged at Wil's heart.

"I'm sorry, Toni, I wasn't even thinking about—"

"I know you weren't." Toni didn't let her go on and refer to the brief affair that had resulted in her daughter and Wil's niece.

The crunch of gravel under the guard's boots stopped Willow from pressing for more details.

"I've got to go, Toni. Don't worry, I'm on it. And I'll let you know ASAP anything I find so that you can do what you need to."

She wasn't going to say the words, voice the sentiment that the guard could overhear.

"Hang on there, Willow. Your only job is to keep your CPA alive and pass any intel you find to me. I'll forward it to the proper authorities, like I did with that car scene and the assailant you chased away. You can last until Wednesday morning, can't you?"

"What happens Wednesday morning?"

"CC's contract with Veronica Clayton terminates. I told her it was a squeeze to get you in, and that I'd do my best to find a replacement. But given what I've dug up, it's a no-go. If you need law enforcement in the meantime, don't hesitate to let me know."

"Wait—why wouldn't I call in a concern directly?" If another harrowing situation like the car attack happened, she didn't want to have to wait for help.

Toni sighed. "Because, sadly, not all LEA are the good guys. We have reliable contacts at each level of the law, from the feds to constables. It's our policy to use them. Unless it's a medical emergency, of course."

"Gotcha." Wil disconnected.

Her older sis wasn't wrong; Wil was no longer on active duty and Jay wasn't her superior, nor did he report to her. But it wasn't professional to get involved with a client, ever. In her thinking, it'd be best to at least terminate the business side of the relationship first.

Holy heck, she was in that mental neighborhood where she'd vowed she wouldn't tread.

"Jay is off-limits," she whispered. If she only had ruby-red slippers to click three times, anything that would stop the way her body reacted around him. If Jay was at all a part of Badger—and she had to face the high probability that he was—she needed to make sure her personal boundaries were tight. And that began with her errant thoughts.

Focus on the assignment.

This was her first civilian face-to-face contract for CC, but it didn't feel all that civilian to her. Mack Logging & Manufacturing wasn't in a combat zone. But what difference did that make if crime syndicates still engaged in assassinations and crimes that were no less deadly than war?

The guard strolled past just as she'd put her phone down

and she returned his short nod, kept her expression neutral. Let him think she was just like him.

I'm not on your side, buddy.

Wil was good at ferreting out the most minuscule detail when it came to cybercrime. As long as she was here, she could put the same skills to use and dig up dirt on the Claytons and their suspected future hostile takeovers. Information that could easily be overlooked by law enforcement as they zeroed in on bringing them to justice.

She'd love to gather enough intelligence to help law enforcement, no question. But most importantly to her, Wil wanted to prevent innocent lives from being lost.

Jay wasn't on the list of innocents, though.

All she had to do was keep him alive until Monday morning.

Not to mention herself.

Chapter 18

Jay knew that Willow would never forget her promise that she wouldn't let him out of her sight long enough to go to the van solo. But a guy could try. He waited until they'd finished off the meat lover's pizza and soda they'd picked up on the way home before broaching the topic.

He looked up from his phone to see her tapping out a text on hers. They again sat on the tarp in what would be the living room, picnic-style.

"Stop staring at me, Jay." She didn't look up from her screen.

"I'm not staring." *Liar.* "I have a proposal for you."

She jerked her head up so quickly her phone fell out of her hand. "What?"

What did she think he was about to ask? Did her sudden flush have anything to do with it? He ignored his lusty wish list.

"It's simple, actually. You stay here and guard the house, all night. You trust me to keep my van and the surrounding woods clear, all night. It's the best way to keep the entire area safe, Wil." He almost called her Willow but bit off the end. Why couldn't Veronica have hired a male former Marine?

"Enough with this." Maybe her rosy cheeks were from

anger, not the desire he'd hoped for. "Just stop, Jay. You're not going into the woods, to your camper, for the rest of the weekend. Not while I'm in charge of keeping you alive."

Willow's eyes flashed with annoyance at his refusal to follow her orders, but tell that to his privates—and not the US Marine kind. The showdown between Badger and their Mexican counterpart was probably no more than forty-eight hours away and yet his attraction to her continued to burn as if he were seventeen and not twice as old, with all the hardened life experience that entailed. Was he self-sabotaging? Was his mind searching for a distraction from what was the culmination of his career to date?

"No offense, Wil, but as far as I'm concerned, once we're on my property, we play by my rules." He held up his hands as her mouth opened. "I get it. Veronica is paying you. You want to complete a successful assignment. But I'm entitled to have some privacy. And I'm not on her clock right now. That accounts for something, doesn't it?"

"No such thing when your life's being threatened." Her chin jutted out and she crossed her arms at her chest. His fingers itched to reach behind her head, tug that sexy ponytail loose, feel the silkiness of her marigold locks, sink said fingers into her nape as he lowered his mouth…

Marigold?

Where the heck had "marigold" come from? Oh yeah, she'd commented on a patch of the flowers in one of his neighbors' front pathways.

His stomach clenched. Now he was hanging on to Willow's words, her every observation.

You were never this enthralled with a woman before, not even your ex. An ex who was five years past and happily married with two kids. Things he couldn't offer a partner, not then and not now. He'd made his choices; Jay was one of the FBI lifers who was married to his job. But tell that to this damning attraction he was fighting tooth and nail.

"But my life isn't threatened out here. Veronica over-reacted, if you ask me. I get that she's concerned about a threat at the workplace, sure. And yeah, we had that road rage stint last evening. But out here?" He opened his arms. "You've seen most of the property, and where my van is. It's safe and far too isolated to make it worth a ticked-off employee's time, don't you agree?"

"Not at all." Her brow wrinkled. "Tell me something, Jay. Did you have a visitor in your camper last night?"

"What? No." It was his turn to pause. "Why do you ask?"

"I encountered someone in the woods."

"Male or female? Were they armed? Did you call it in to your boss, or the local PD?" The queries flew out of his mouth. Too quickly.

But she didn't give any indication of finding his sudden interest in law enforcement surprising.

"Don't worry, Jay, no one else knows about them." Her sharp tone made his scalp prickle. She thought he was a bad guy. One of the Badgers. Or did she think he was part of the Mexican cartel?

"What do you know about Mack that you're not telling me, Wil?" he asked.

She held out her hands in a beseeching gesture. "What's there to know? The Claytons have owned it for almost seven decades. Veronica took over CEO functions when Cal Clayton became ill. His two sons by a previous marriage manage overall operations and sales."

"Was that on the first page of your internet search or did you read the company website?" He opted for the easiest defense with distraction. "And what does that have to do with my going out to my camper tonight?"

Her brow arched and her lips twisted into an expression that he read as disbelieving. Yeah, she was on to him, but how much exactly, he couldn't be sure.

"Tell you what, Jay. You can go out to your camper, no problem. As long as I'm with you."

"Deal." He should be happy, relieved. All he wanted to do was tell her that he wasn't one of them. He was like the men she'd served with. A good guy.

Good guys didn't drool after a possible target. Problem was, he no longer saw Willow as someone he'd have to take out if need be. Instead, she'd become the one person he wanted to protect from all of this.

She wasn't an enemy; she was technically an innocent, unwittingly hired by a Badger. Except Willow wasn't innocent, not the way her eyes silently begged him to kiss her. She felt this thing between them, too. And she'd resisted it.

Why couldn't he?

Wil shoved her necessary gear for the evening into her backpack as she knelt on the living room floor. Jay was getting whatever he needed from his room.

She didn't believe for one minute that Jay intended to allow her inside what she'd considered a man cave on wheels. Now, she wasn't sure what that van was used for. If Jay was part of Veronica's plans to take over the Mexican cartel, a real possibility that Wil had to accept no matter how hard he made her insides swoon, then the van might have all the evidence any LEA would need to not only prevent a showdown, but obtain an eventual conviction.

As she hoisted up her backpack, complete with a sleeping bag, she bit back a grin. In truth, on the physical level this gig was far less complicated than the cybercrimes she was familiar with, and definitely a lot more cush than her military field experiences.

It was the thinking that was driving her nuts. The constant worry that at any minute Jay could pull a weapon on her, or that they'd be in the middle of a firefight, wore at her composure.

Having the hots for Jay didn't help. But now that she knew how bad he really was, her hormones had no choice but to take a hike.

Footsteps sounded behind her, and she looked over her shoulder as Jay approached from his bedroom. His gaze swept over her and landed on the backpack, but not before heat rose up her neck and into her cheeks. What did it say about her that she was damnably attracted to a criminal?

You're human.

Thank goodness for Toni's words, or she wouldn't be able to see past beating herself up.

She braced herself for Jay's criticism of her gear, prepared to explain yet again that as long as she was getting paid to maintain his safety, he wasn't leaving her sight. Save for the obvious bathroom and shower breaks.

"You have a waterproof jacket in there?" He nodded at her pack. "It's supposed to drop in temps and rain."

"The rain isn't getting here until tomorrow morning." She didn't bother to tell him that she had all she'd need in just about any situation packed into her rucksack. Or that she was going to sleep inside the van if need be, whatever it took to keep an eye on him while in a secure place. She needed a decent night's rest to do her job, especially if the situation blew up before she left on Monday morning.

He shrugged. "Your call. I suggest we go through my bedroom, head out on the deck. I've got the house lights on timers, so it'll appear I'm still here."

"Following you." She kept her thoughts private, only after biting her inside cheek. It took every bit of her self-discipline to not point out the obvious: Jay was as concerned about his safety out here as he was at Mack headquarters. Otherwise why worry if anyone saw him leave via the side entry, or even the front door?

Toni's information should have been the cold dousing she'd needed to face facts. But no, she'd needed this affirmation that Jay was a dirty player in this sick syndicate cat-and-mouse. Jay was one of the bad guys, knee-deep in a quagmire of potentially spilled blood, and she stood alongside him.

"Careful, they're more slippery than last night." He spoke over his shoulder from the third step down.

"Gotcha."

She'd never let him know what she knew. Not until she gleaned valuable information she could in turn pass on to Toni. When it came to a fight for justice, Wil was all in.

The irony that she and Jay both were keeping secrets from one another wasn't lost on her as they pretended to be amiable. The high-level gamesmanship was to be expected, she silently reasoned. What was unexpected, however, was the tight swirl of disappointment in her belly.

Oh, boy. She'd gotten herself into serious emotional risk in a very short time. And it was only her first "side job" for CC. A side hustle that could become life-altering at any moment.

Focused on getting down the stairs, she was caught up short at the bottom when she ran into Jay. He turned around.

"You okay?" Concern crinkled the skin between his brows. It seemed so genuine!

"I'm good. Wasn't looking."

If you only knew.

She took the rest of the trek two steps behind Jay, and all along the forest path she kept alert for any sign of danger. Three deer and one porcupine were the only beings that crossed their path, announced by Jay and spotted by her as they traipsed into the safety of the underbrush.

It came more naturally for her to lead, but Jay knew the path better than she. Hell, he'd made this path, from what she'd surmised. Or had it been created by another member of the Badger syndicate? Was "Jay's" camper getaway van actually a crash pad for the bad guys?

Shaking her head to clear her mind, she reminded herself to stay present, stay alert. And silently vowed she'd let Toni know this was her first and final personal protection detail. In fact, no more personal jobs, period. Cybercrime was far more challenging and posed far less risk to her self-esteem. Computers didn't hurt her feelings, make her heart heavy.

They don't make your insides burn with desire, either.

They hiked the mile through the forest in silence and he told himself it was just as well, that he didn't want to know one more thing about her. Jay wasn't one for small talk even if holding a cold glass of his favorite dark ale and sitting with his work team. He'd always preferred discussing the things that mattered. His passions: Justice. Criminology, which he'd excelled at in college. Maybe how he'd outfitted a bare-bones Ford transit van into a house on wheels—and a covert FBI agent office—all by himself, in his spare time.

He'd caught glimpses of the same drive for excellence in the depths of Willow's hazel eyes. It was why he was physically attracted to her, he figured. Okay, that, and her hot bod.

You shouldn't even be thinking about Willow.

Viewing Willow as more than anything but a thorn in

his side as he attempted to wrap up a case that had cost the agency two agents to date, countless hours of manpower and the sacrifice of his own personal life these last two years wasn't just dangerous.

It was lethal.

So silence was his choice, and apparently Willow's, too, as they said no more than "watch it, root" or "thicket of poison oak on your left."

He had to credit her with being in excellent shape, as she kept up with him step for step and he never heard her breathing. He listened for her footfalls behind him, purely out of reflex, to make sure she was still with him.

When they reached the clearing, he veered straight for the van, knowing the conflict his words were going to stir up. He stopped at the van's side entrance, placed one hand on the handle, the other on the padlock that unlocked with a retina scan.

The eye scan allowed him to utter the words he knew she'd resent, and fight, without looking at her. His plan was to get himself inside before she went ballistic. If he didn't need to be inside the van to access his secure systems so badly, he'd call his action chicken shit. But tonight, it was a mandatory measure. A matter of survival.

"I'm glad you're okay with staying out here and keeping the perimeter clear. I'll be safe inside, and I'll come out in a few hours." The padlock unlocked and he opened the door.

"Nice try, slick. I don't have a problem with you not wanting me in the van with you, but I have to check out the inside before you go in, and I need to see every egress—er, exit route." Willow was in Marine mode. It gave him comfort that she could take care of herself. But it didn't erase the deep, instinctive need he had to protect her. A need, like his desire for her, that had to be quashed.

"Can you let me by, please?" She was unaware of his inner turmoil. A model bodyguard. Who was about to go into what until now had been his inner sanctum.

No way.

There wasn't anything she'd see that was a security risk. He always cleaned up whatever he was working on, and the van had zero evidence of his real identity. A few of his systems would look like simple computer CPUs to an inexperienced, non-LE type. But Willow was a freaking cyber expert. She'd know better than anyone what kind of work his systems were capable of.

Fortunately, that particular hardware was under heavy blankets and behind storage cabinet doors. Willow was looking for an intruder and would skip any space that couldn't fit a human, he'd bet. But he couldn't do the deep dive into the reports from his team in DC with Willow right next to him in the van. Because there wasn't enough room to keep anything from her knowing gaze.

You're not worried about the systems. Admit it.

The greatest threat to this takedown, hell, to his sanity, was Willow. The last thing he needed was to be cooped up in his trailer with the one woman who'd turned his head since he'd gone undercover. The single woman he'd ever felt this strong a pull toward.

Jay let out a breath, turned and faced Willow. Night was gaining fast, but the remaining twilight was enough to make out details he'd best forget.

Her ball cap was pulled low on her brow, but she tilted her head back far enough to meet his gaze, and he fought like hell to not drown in it. It'd be too easy to disregard all of his silent vows and make love to her on the spot. Auburn tendrils that had escaped her ponytail rested on her cheek like loose corkscrews. His hands curled into tight fists, fighting the temptation to wrap the strands around his fingers as he pulled her close.

Willow took a step back, kept her eyes level with his. It was as if she sensed his private desire, the emotional quicksand they both stood too close to.

"Jay, come on. We've gone over this already. I'm your keeper—" she pointed her thumb at her chest "—until either your CEO tells me I'm not, or my boss replaces me with another CC agent. There isn't any wiggle room here. Trust me, if there was, I'd be the first to use it."

"I'm not going to be able to do what I need to with you breathing over my shoulder, Wil."

Her eyes narrowed in the swiftly darkening evening. A leathery flap of wings sounded and they both looked up to see the distinct profile of a great horned owl as it left its roost overhead to hunt. The wingspan was impressive, the fact that they both paused to watch the magnificent sight even more so.

"I saw him last night, too." Her reverent tone mirrored the awe that the raptors triggered in him.

"There was a pair of them until a few weeks ago, and a juvenile."

She turned back to him, shoved her hands in the pockets of her fleece pullover. Her expression had lost the sternness of seconds ago, and his gut muscles unclenched in response. As if the owl's flight had carried their antagonism away upon its broad wings.

"Look, Jay. I don't want to fight. You're absolutely right. You need your space." She paused, and he imagined her unspoken thoughts. *I need my space, too.* "I don't have to stay inside your van, but I do have to clear it. Let me do that, and I'll happily stay out here and wait for you to do whatever it is you're so intent on accomplishing. I'm prepared to sleep out here, but I'd rather not. We're safer in the house, frankly."

That's what you think. If Veronica's goons came calling, it wouldn't be with anything less than automatic weapons, maybe a grenade or five. He kept his thoughts to himself, though. They'd wasted enough time standing out here, and he had work to do.

"It's a deal then. Go ahead and do what you've got to do." He opened the door wide. Before he could stop himself, he waved her inside and bowed. "It's all yours, as you wish. You've got thirty seconds." He growled the last bit, not intending to, but standing this close to Willow, spending the entire day with her, plus yesterday… It was all adding up. The constant barrage of awareness of her, her voice, her scent…it had created chinks in his defenses. Small cracks that were too close to exploding.

Please let this job be over before I do something stupid. Except it wouldn't be stupid to get involved with Willow— it'd be deadly, mostly for her.

A soft laugh escaped her lips. The sexy sound hit him square in the solar plexus, but instead of taking his breath away as a punch would, it exploded into white-hot lust that shot straight to his groin.

It was a good thing he was bent over as she climbed up the easy step into the van, because he was certain she'd be able to see the evidence of her effect on him.

"It sounds like we might have the same taste in movies." She'd caught his nod to *The Princess Bride* with 'as you wish,' the oft repeated phrase of the hero to the heroine. A warm pulse spiraled in his belly that she 'got' him.

"Listen, Jay, I'm not prepared to have either of us die, so give me a full minute to do my job." She wasn't in a bargaining mood, but her tone had softened, and she'd thrown her version of a movie quote back at him with a riff off of "prepare to die," from the same movie. Which turned the warmth in his center into a heat he knew he could never satisfy with her, no matter how tempting.

"Go ahead." He wasn't in a place to argue with her. The animosity that had plagued them on the hike here had dissipated. It was actually a good thing that he'd agreed to let her clear the van. He needed the time to remind himself that he was in the middle of a potentially lethal undercover operation, not at all in any kind of space to entertain his desire to take Willow O'Malley to bed.

While she moved about the van, Jay used the centering techniques he'd learned while working alongside Navy SEALs to refocus. Within two deep breaths he was back to himself.

You'll never be the same after knowing Willow.

Before he could spin back up over the unwelcome thought, Willow reappeared in the threshold.

"I thought you fell in the cassette toilet. That was closer to forty-five seconds, for the record." He made it a point to look at his watch.

"All clear." She ignored his verbal prod. "And for the record? I'm not a fan of cassette toilets, as much as I love the freedom a camper van affords a traveler."

"Why is that?" he asked. "I think the camper van's toilet is ingenious. It literally snaps out of the bottom of the camper, and with its handle and wheels, it's just like carry-on luggage."

"Yeah, except you're not wheeling onto an aircraft for an exotic location. You're taking it to the waste site to dump the contents." Her expression soured and he laughed.

"My, my, this is a pleasant surprise." He grinned at her. "The perfect Marine has a flaw."

"I don't think a repulsion to dumping human waste is a deal breaker when it comes to keeping you alive." Her serious, professional expression was back in place. *Pity.* "You're free to head inside. I'll be waiting right here, except for when I walk the perimeter of the clearing. If you happen to hear anything—like a gunshot—get on the floor and stay down until I tell you it's okay to come out." She placed her hand on his shoulder and hopped down, then strode to where she'd dropped her backpack and collapsible camping stool. And damn if his shoulder didn't feel the hot imprint of her hand through his layers of outerwear.

"See you in a bit, then."

He entered the van, shut and locked the door behind him, then willed his mind to focus on the research and reports he needed to complete.

The touch of her hand on his shoulder had effectively branded him. It reminded him that he could ignore it all he wanted to, but his attraction to Willow wasn't going away.

Neither was the threat from the Badger and Mexican syndicates.

"Work with what will kill you first," he said to himself as he booted up his systems. The stress of prolonged undercover work was getting to him, no question. Because his gut screamed that Willow would kill him the quickest.

Don't you mean break your heart?

He snorted. Just as lethal.

Chapter 19

Wil thought about using her portable LED lantern's red bulb—night-vision mode—but her infantry instincts kept her sitting silently, in the middle of the woods, listening to the forest as the world went to sleep and the night creatures awakened.

She figured that the risk of Jay being tracked out here without her being alerted was minimal. Unless the stalker was an expert hiker, which she doubted. Whoever had tried to run them off the road hadn't reappeared, and if the driver was the same person she'd chased off the property last night, they'd know that coming after Jay meant they had to get through her first.

From what Toni had relayed and what Willow had suspected all along, the chances that Jay was simply a CPA were nil. He had to be part of either Veronica's syndicate, or more possibly, the Mexican cartel that she wanted to take over. From all she'd learned from working cybercrime for CC these past few months, organized crime worked as if they were their own governments. Laws unto themselves, solely for the benefit of the syndicate. The motive was always and only to line the pockets of the kingpins. With zero care about human suffering. Period.

Willow had gotten a few insights into drug and human

trafficking while working military operations, mostly in developing nations.

She was forever grateful to the transglobal agencies that worked 24-7 to destroy human trafficking. Because as much as she was a Marine forever, and would do whatever it took to get a job done, she knew her limits. Witnessing the abuse and often murder of innocent children and women at the hands of the evilest of human beings on the planet wasn't something she ever felt she had the guts for. In her estimation, it would kill her soul.

Yet here she was, no longer in uniform, but possibly in the midst of a malevolence the likes of which she'd never experienced. Facing down a criminal syndicate was to her more difficult than ferreting out a cybercriminal. The in-person syndicate appeared 'normal' on the surface. Veronica wore nice clothes, lived in a beautiful part of the Pacific Northwest, employed a few hundred local employees in a legitimate business. Veronica also had a definite charm, and if she wasn't such an observant person Wil knows she may have missed the threatening undercurrent she'd sensed coming off the CEO. But no matter how pretty the frosting, Veronica's 'cake'—her actions—was no less violent than a warlord's.

"Just great, girl. Nice career change." She spoke to herself under her breath and looked up at the clear night sky.

A snap sounded to her right, shooting her to her feet. She pulled her NVGs over her eyes, grabbed her weapon and waited.

A loud voice sounded, but it was in the van. She listened. It wasn't a cry of help, but sounded more like Jay was yelling at a football game. Her shoulders relaxed. He wasn't in distress. Maybe watching a game was how he unwound?

No matter. She'd definitely heard something, someone,

in the woods. Standing out here wasn't giving her any advantage, so she quickly retreated to behind the small boulder in front of the van.

And continued to wait.

Guilt clawed at Jay's better judgment. He knew he had to block Willow out, let her do whatever she had to outside. It wouldn't have worked with her inside, with him. She could have sat up front, in the passenger seat, where she couldn't see his computer displays. But she could walk back here at any time—

Stop. He'd just wasted the last five minutes going over all the reasons Willow couldn't be so close to him. Why was he doubting his own judgment? Willow had accepted his need for space. Why couldn't he? He had a job to do.

And yet...

"Willow O'Malley is the real deal."

Janice's words echoed in his mind, their significance sending reverberations of excitement deep inside his chest. He was leaving her out there as though she were indeed a part-time security guard. With no sense of respect for her time served. His father had been a veteran, also a Marine, and had died for his country. Jay and his brother and mother had been left without a father, husband and years of family memories. He'd been seventeen when Pop's unit had been surrounded. Pop had made it initially, only to die of his injuries once back in the States.

What would Pop say now?

He swore. To distract himself from his monkey brain and to reassure himself that Willow was perfectly fine, he called up the live security video feeds.

No sign of anyone around the house, or on the wooded path, where he'd strategically placed small motion-detector cameras. He clicked to the camera with a full view of the van.

Willow's camping chair was empty. But he made out her form behind the boulder, placing her ten feet from the van's door. She crouched low, looked to be wearing NVGs and held her weapon in both hands. He'd bet the safety was off. What had she heard? He stood and clicked on the next closest camera, the one that encompassed the clearing as well as the last ten yards of the forest path.

Blood drained from his face. There, in a definitive shooter posture, wearing NVGs and aiming toward the van, was a large figure, probably male. Willow was no more than ten feet from the van, but it could have been the Grand Canyon. He couldn't protect her unless he got her inside.

"Damn it!" This time he shouted. Let Willow hear him; let the bastard she'd alerted to hear him, too.

Willow froze. She'd definitely heard a loud male voice again. Jay's. And again, it was from inside the van. She let out her breath.

What the heck was Jay doing in there? Suddenly, thoughts of all the things that could be happening to him assaulted her imagination. Screw waiting for some harmless porcupine to scare her again. She stood and ran to the van.

But as she came upon the side door, it flew open, Jay's inimitable form backlit by glowing light.

"Jay!" His name tore from her lips.

"Willow." Guttural—dare she say tortured?

"What's wrong? Are you—are you alone?" she asked. She shoved the NVGs up onto her head to peer into the dimly lit van. Was there an intruder behind him, ready to kill while she watched—

"Yes, of course I am. You cleared the van, remember?"

"And I saw there's an ingress, um, a way in, with that skylight."

"I know what an ingress is. And I keep it locked, for what it's worth. Look, I might be a bean counter, but I'm not a complete idiot." He leaned against the minimal door-jamb. She felt the burn of his gaze on her, as it was impossible to see his expression with the lack of moonlight.

She crossed her arms over her chest. "I'm not an idiot, either, Ja—"

Bam, bam, bam.

It all happened so fast. The unmistakable sound of muf-fled gunfire, Jay's hands reaching for her as she jumped up to protect him, Jay rolling her over and springing back up onto his haunches and slamming the side door shut, lock-ing it. He dragged her by the upper arm, shoved her to the passenger seat floor.

"Cover for me!" He barked the order as he slid into the driver's seat and started the engine.

Bullets hit the side of the van and she prayed the tires remained intact as she did exactly what he said. It was what she'd have told him to do if she'd been driving. There wasn't time to question Jay's orders or her responses. They were in a race to save their lives.

She felt with her fingers for the window control, and as soon as there was a pause in the gunfire, she hit it, lower-ing the window, and returned fire.

Jay threw the van into gear and floored it. He made cer-tain the head- and brake lights were disengaged—a feature he was particularly proud of—and used his night-vision goggles to see through the windshield. With zero hesita-tion he made a 270-degree turn onto the path he'd mowed two weeks ago, after he'd established the best location for the van as the showdown with Badger became imminent.

Willow fired her pistol until he made the turn, putting them out of direct line of fire. "Talk to me." He couldn't risk looking away from the roughly hewn road, which he'd deliberately made very twisty and unintuitive.

"I can't tell if I got them." He heard her climb into the seat, the distinct clicks of reloading a handgun.

"Stay down!" He fought against the instinct to shove her back into the wheel well, but the steering wheel required both hands. Each turn appeared to dead-end into either a thick copse of trees or the edge of a cliff. The tributary that ran behind the densest part of the woods had several sharp drop-offs that would prove deadly to the uninitiated. Fortunately for them, Jay had committed the route to memory when he created it.

Bam, bam, bam.

More bullets hit the van, this time sounding from the back. A motor revved behind them.

"Take them out—use the back door if you have to!" he yelled over the engine, the branches scraping the sides of the van, the roar of a motorcycle behind them.

"I can see him from here." Willow fired again. This time he risked a glance to his right. Willow was hanging out of the passenger window.

In one hundred feet, the road was about to make another too-sharp turn, right at the edge of a cliff. "Get back in! Now!" He took his foot off the gas pedal.

But it was too late. He had to make the turn or kill both of them in a free fall into the river hundreds of feet below.

"If I open the back doors, we're both dead. There's a motorbike right behind us!" Willow shot the update over her

shoulder as she hung, her waist atop the glass pane, half-
way out the passenger window, firing back at their stalker.

"Get back inside."

"Can't," she yelled as she fired off two more rounds.
The single headlight remained.

Was this how she was going to die?

As soon as she had the thought, Jay made a turn. Her
arm hit the side of the window frame, and her weapon was
knocked out of her hand and into the darkness. It was all in
slow motion as her body floated, and a deep recess of her
brain wondered if she was going to fly off into the trees.

So when she felt a sharp tug on her waist, forcing her
back into the van with such impact that her head hit the
roof above her seat, what she witnessed didn't register right
away.

The single light that identified their attacker didn't make
the turn with them, but kept going, straight, straight. The
engine grew louder for a split second as she watched the
light pause in midair. And then it dropped straight down,
disappearing. Jay jerked the van to a stop right before the
sound of a distant splash reached her ears.

They'd done it! They'd lost the shooter.

She turned to Jay, eager to see her relief if not outright
triumph reflected in his gaze. But she couldn't see his reaction. Not because of the dark. The glow of the dash lights
illuminated the cabin, each of them, making everything
seem otherworldly. The silence warned her first. Not one
word, not one relieved groan from Jay that they were safe.

It took her a few heartbeats to assess and accept the situation. Jay had no response because he wasn't conscious.
His head lay back on his seat, and his eyes were closed
with a dark stain on his lids. She followed the unmistakable dark path of blood to the wound—another inky spot

that she instinctively knew was a mean gash. The kind of wound that shot cold fear through her belly.

Had Jay taken a bullet?

"Stop," Jay protested forcefully. Or, thought he had, but all he heard was a strained voice barely above a whisper. Was that his voice?

When the cold, wet cloth or whatever the unwelcome object was continued to swipe at his forehead, Jay had to face facts. That soft squeak had been his voice, and judging from how his head felt like a watermelon stuffed inside an egg, the person leaning over him was cleaning a wound of some sort.

"Stay still." Soft but firm.

Willow.

"I'm fine," he croaked.

"Sure you are. That's why you've got a cut clear down to your skull and you just threw up." She sounded relieved.

He struggled to lift his lids. A blurry outline of her, but he'd know Willow anywhere. "Thanks. I'll... I'll get us going again, don't worry."

"I'm not worried." He heard the rip of paper a second before she was touching his head again, right over his eye where it hurt like hell. "These butterfly bandages are going to have to do until we get you to an ER."

"I'm not going to a hospital."

A pause in her ministrations, a quick intake of breath. Something in him stirred, and his mind replayed their almost-kiss. His memory hadn't been affected by the bonk to his head, at least. Neither had his—

"Why no ER, Jay? Afraid of being arrested?"

"Hardly." There. His voice was coming back. "What happened to motorcycle man?"

"What do you remember?"

"Do not play with me, Willow. I'm not some bad guy you have to worry about. The dude who was firing at us? He's who you need to worry about it. Oh, shit—was I shot?" Belatedly he pieced together the events of the last moments before he blacked out.

"No, it doesn't look like it. I thought it might be a bullet, too, but from the way this—" she held up a portable rechargeable battery pack "—is shaped, I'm thinking you had it in your sun visor and it flew loose when you made that last turn."

"I don't usually keep heavy things up there, but I wasn't driving the van…wait, I shut off the engine after that turn…" That was all he remembered.

"You didn't shut it off, but you did shift into Park. Good thing, or we'd be stuck in between cedar trees. Permanently."

He pushed her away and moved to sit up. She was still bent over him in the confines of the van's cab, and he felt her hand immediately press on his chest, forcing him to slow down. And no wonder. The minute he was upright the windshield wavered in front of him and he had to grip the steering wheel with his eyes screwed tight, breathing through his mouth, to keep from vomiting again.

Her hand moved to his shoulder, where she gave him a reassuring squeeze. He heard her steps as she made her way around the back of the camper, heard the refrigerator door slam shut a few seconds later. The pop of a soda can never sounded so painful. He really must have taken a solid conk.

"Good thing you have a nice stash of drinks in here." She pressed a cold bottle into his palm. "It's ginger ale. Sip it slowly. I think you have a concussion."

"Ya think?" He didn't open his eyes as he gulped the cool liquid.

"Easy there, champ." Her dry tone forced a small laugh from him, and no matter how crappy he felt in this moment, he knew they'd be just fine.

They'd?

Nausea threatened again and he put his head on the steering wheel, allowing the bandaged cut to hit the solid form. He involuntarily sucked in a harsh breath as he winced at the pain.

"Stay in an upright position, or lean back. Going forward like that won't help the closing. We don't want that doing any more than oozing."

"Sounds like Marine Corps first aid training."

"Oorah!" The response exploded in the van and he groaned while Willow laughed. The headache from her shout was worth it to hear her laugh, a rich sound that could heal all the world's problems.

He was so screwed.

"I know you're going to say no—"

"No."

"But hear me out." Firmer. Her no-nonsense tone was back. "We can't stay parked here. We're sitting ducks. I assume you're the one who carved out this road to the clearing? And maybe you thought you were the only one who knows about it? We know that's not true now. Whoever was chasing us knew it. They took the turns too easily to not have found it."

"They're dead." He remembered hearing the splash right before everything turned black.

"Yes, that person is, but I doubt they're operating alone. If you're being targeted by an environmentalist radical or another person with a deep grudge against Mack, there are more where he or she came from."

There was an unspoken question in her statement that he chose to ignore but knew he had to answer, and soon.

Could he trust Willow with his real identity?

"You're going to ride shotgun and I'm driving." Willow braced for Jay's protest.

"As much as it kills me to admit this to you, you're right. You need to drive. But can we establish where we're headed?"

She'd thought about it while tending to him. Praying that he'd wake up, even though she'd seen head wounds before and knew they were bloody, and he was still breathing, so she hadn't feared the worst. Not at a practical level.

But her heart…her insides had flipped in the most sickening manner in those thirty seconds or so that Jay had been out. When she'd shone her phone's light on the sharp-edged mini CB unit she assumed Jay used for comms backup, she realized it had been stored in the visor and flown out when Jay made his sudden stop. The corner of the metal box had nailed his temple. The hit could have killed him. In those brief moments her thoughts had traversed dark terrain. A place where Jay no longer existed.

How a man she'd known for barely forty-eight hours had become so important to her, she didn't know or understand. The downside was that he was a criminal. On the bright side, his well-being was still her responsibility, so anything she did for him she did for Cascade Confidential, for Toni.

Talk about situational ethics.

"I need to verify my plans with my boss, but with CC approval, we're going on the lam for a bit. I think it's important for you to disappear until whatever is going on with Mack is over."

"Not an option." He spoke as he gingerly but definitely moved into the passenger seat. She sat in the bench seat at the tiny café table behind the driver's seat. He'd left the table up when they had to flee, and hadn't broken it down and slid it behind the seat, a feature she knew about from her other friends who had camper vans. He hadn't lied to her. Jay definitely hadn't been expecting to be on the move tonight.

"Why not?" Willow tried to sound neutral as her thoughts screamed at her.

In the very short inspection she'd given the inside of his van, she'd seen enough of the high-tech equipment to know that Jay was either in so thick with some very bad guys—bad enough to have deep pockets, which would be needed for all the different systems this van was loaded down with—or he was working for a government entity of some sort. Whether it was the United States or another nation, she couldn't be absolutely certain. And damn it, she wanted to be certain. She wanted to believe with all her heart that Jay was a good guy, that he was working to dismantle what Toni had described as "one of the slickest and deadliest crime syndicates in North America, ever."

Beliefs and desires weren't facts, though. When it came to work and her professional standards, Wil didn't know how to deal in anything but the absolute truth. Her siblings teased her about being too black and white because she wasn't comfortable with gray areas. She couldn't be as a cyberwarrior.

It wasn't that she doubted what she'd do if need be. If Jay was part of a crime syndicate, or a foreign nation supporting one, she'd cuff him herself, and not in a sexy way. No question, Wil would turn Jay in, in a heartbeat.

That wasn't the question. If the truth proved Jay was on the wrong side of the law, the unknown was far more personal, something she could never express. Would turning Jay in break her heart?

Holy hell. She wasn't in too deep here. She was drowning.

Chapter 20

Wil didn't give Jay a chance to respond to her request to know why he didn't think they could go on the lam. Instead, she walked to the back of the van, giving Jay some time to reconsider his response. She used the moment to secure the blinds on the windshields and shades on rear side windows so that she could safely illuminate the inside of the camper without being seen outside. She wasn't as concerned about anyone finding them so soon after the motorcycle stalker had met his or her demise, but she wasn't taking any chances.

She clicked on the overhead lighting, which placed the mini banquette in a soft glow. The van's bed wasn't apparent. She hadn't noticed a Murphy bed, nor were there sofas that converted to sleeping areas. Instead, locked cupboards lined both sides of the van, and she'd spied an office chair in the far back, in the place where she'd expected a stall shower. A pile of blankets was in another unlocked closet, under which she'd found two CPUs. In ordinary circumstances, where she'd believe Jay was truly a CPA, the extra computers wouldn't have fazed her. But they'd fired off warning bells as she silently added up what little she did know about Jay, and what she'd witnessed while protecting him.

But she didn't focus on any of that now. "There. That's better. Are you up to moving a little more? I think you'll get a better chance at resting back here, and I want to close the blinds across the cab."

He grunted his response as he slowly stood, but remained hunched in the cab, as he was too tall for it. His hands gripped the back of the driver and passenger seats and he took a long pause, his face forward but his eyes closed.

"I need you to let go of the driver's seat for a sec so I can turn it around."

"Do you own a camper van?" Spoken through gritted teeth, revealing his discomfort.

"No, but I grew up camping, and several friends used their reenlistment bonuses to purchase camper vans just like yours." *Without the cloak-and-dagger computers.* She kept her tone light, instinct telling her that the best way to Jay's truth was not necessarily a direct offense or interrogation. He needed to be able to trust that she'd support his wishes, no matter what she really planned to do.

What she'd *have* to do.

"Okay." Said as he breathed out with force, his eyes squeezed shut.

"If you're dizzy—" she began to offer.

"Stop." The syllable reverberated like a bark in the tiny space. It at once offered her relief and ire. Relief that Jay was getting back on his feet, literally, and ire that he hadn't let her in any more than he'd had to. They'd just outwitted a killer, and yet Jay was acting as if it made no difference as to what their next moves would be.

As if she didn't exist. It reminded her of the way Derek had intimated she was no more than a glorified mall cop. A rent-a-cop.

She watched as he opened his eyes and gingerly lowered himself onto the driver's seat, now facing the small table. She sat on the bench seat, directly across from him.

"You haven't answered my question, Jay. Why can't you disappear for a couple of days, call in sick? Lie. Say you tested positive for the 'vid. There's no supervisor on the planet who'd make you come to work with full-on COVID. It'd give you at least five days to wait out whatever's going on with Mack."

"No can do." He growled his response, and his expression had cleared from the initial dazed look he'd given her right after the conk on his head. "You've met Veronica, Derek. Do you think they give a flying flip about whether I'm sick or not?"

Rage blossomed, flooding her system with both heat and grit.

"Enough of the BS, Jay. Why don't you come clean with me? I can't protect you if I don't know who you really are." She regretted the antagonism she couldn't keep out of her tone. Jay was like a grizzly bear. Confrontation with one rarely ended well.

"Once I tell you, that's it, Willow. There's no going back." Softly spoken, but his gaze seared through her.

Her breath caught and her face grew hot, then cold, as her pulse thumped in her ears. She swallowed, pressed on.

"So what is it, Jay? Tell me the truth." She was proud of how level she sounded, how strong her voice was considering her insides quivered with terror. Was he going to try to kill her instead of admitting he was on the wrong team?

He sighed. "I'm only telling you this because I've had you vetted. I know you're the real deal, Willow. I trust you."

"Who the hell are you?"

"I'm an FBI agent."

Chapter 21

"FBI." Willow's whisper didn't soften the accusation in her eyes. He didn't know if she believed him, and he knew he shouldn't give a damn if she did or didn't. If it was anyone else, he wouldn't care. But it was Willow. Something deep inside him needed her to know that he was on the right side of the law, that he played on the same team as her.

And so he waited, unable to follow up his admission. Silence settled between them as he allowed his admission to soak in, gave Willow the space she deserved to make her own decision about how they'd proceed.

Proceed with what?

He ignored his ever-present FBI training. Just for this single moment.

"You shouldn't." Her words broke the quiet.

"Shouldn't what?"

"Trust me. How do you know I'm not on Veronica's side?" Her gaze locked on his, and he saw the way her pupils contrasted with her irises. The way they dilated. Bedroom eyes…

"I have to admit, it makes sense. I mean, everything clicks into place. How your house seems as if it hasn't been lived in for so much longer than you told me you've owned it. Why you spend so many hours—every night, in fact—

here in the van, far from the house. And of course, all of your equipment—let me guess, behind those locked cabinets is state-of-the-art tech gear to monitor Mack, keep tabs on the security cameras that are installed on the house? And I assume you have them in the woods, too, since you came out of the van at the exact moment the shooter opened fire?"

"Yes." His gut tightened. This was like one of those trust fall exercises he'd seen in the movies—nothing he'd ever participated in—except he was the one falling backward, and he had no idea if Willow wanted to catch him or help him break his neck. No matter that her current job description demanded she save him.

"You knew I was legit, Jay. God, is that even your real name?" She looked away, and he knew he had to be patient, wait for her to absorb his truth.

"I'm Jay, but it's Jayden Lambert, not Jay Jones."

"You knew I was a Marine." She went on as if she no longer cared what he said his name was. "I've no doubt you did a background check on me deep enough to clear me for TS/SCI." Top Secret/Special Compartmented Intelligence was the highest level of government clearance. She used the agency vernacular he was so familiar with. Another reason they'd make a great team. Their common understanding of red tape, the law and code they were both expected to live up to. And the rules that could be broken in the right circumstances.

"I had no choice, Wil." He didn't mention that he'd had files on every single person working at Mack headquarters for months. The US military didn't perform any kind of operation or collect information on US civilians, period. As FBI, he played by a different script. He had to admit he was trying to protect her, too. The less she knew about the crime syndicate, the better. Just in case.

You'll never let anyone take her.

Willow's gaze came back to his, her eyes bright, clear.

"Either you're a very, very bad guy with a helluva lot of funding and know-how, or—" She faltered, clearly at a crossroads. Was this going to be the same fork-in-the-road decision for her as for him? All or nothing?

"Stop thinking, Wil. Trust me." As the request left his mouth, he saw it for what it was. A plea.

He wanted—no!—he *needed* Willow. In every way imaginable.

Willow stared at Jay until she had to look away, had to keep her bearings, as the truth suddenly seemed so obvious. Jay was FBI. A good guy. But she couldn't let him off easily. CC demanded her prudence, and her heart needed to avoid anything that would shatter it.

"Forgive me if I don't take your word for it, Jay. I'm used to a world where enemy foreign governments constantly hack into our systems and enemy foreign agents pose as us worldwide. How do I know you and your systems are legit?"

"Here." He stood and immediately reached for a wall. "Whoa, still a bit topsy-turvy." He sat back down. "Uh, see the shelf over the cab? Get my laptop—it's under the deflated river raft."

Her instinct was to refuse, but she did as he requested. "What else do you have up here?" She peered into the cubbyhole, one of many in the camper van.

"There's a bag of trail mix with dark chocolate in that one container that looks like dog food. Get that, and I'll take another soda from the fridge if you don't mind."

She set the tin in front of him, got them each a beverage. He'd logged into his laptop and turned it around so that

Willow could see the screen. It displayed a government system's known login site, requesting the correct credentials.

"Right. So that you can capture my personal identification data?" She let out a harsh laugh.

He flipped the computer around again, moved his fingers with the same impossibly quick motions she used herself, then flipped it back.

"Look," he said.

Jay had logged himself in and opened his profile. Jay Lambert, special agent, current assignment… UD. Undisclosed. That made sense. But this could still be a fake account, made to mimic the system she knew intimately, as did every other military cyberwarfare expert. Tentatively, then with more confidence, she maneuvered around the system. It certainly looked legit, with none of the usual telltale signs of being a fake.

"You could have been grooming me all along." She couldn't let go, not yet.

"I could have. But I wasn't." He spoke quietly, waiting for her to process the truth.

"I really thought you were part of the syndicate." She whispered her last. He reached for her—

Crack. The sound outside made both of them jump in their seats.

"Get down!" Jay's reflexes hadn't been damaged as he hit the main breaker to the battery power and put his hand on her head. They slid off the bench seats and onto the van floor, crouching low behind the cab, using the driver's and passenger's seats for protection.

Not that a car seat of any type would stop a bullet.

"Do you think—"

His palm, rough yet gentle, pressed over her mouth as he raised his index finger to his lips. *Shh.*

Cedar mingled with clove and what she knew was undeniably Jay's musk. The heat from his hand remained after he removed it, obviously satisfied that she understood the need for silence.

He thought their attacker was still out there.

As her vision adjusted to the dark inside of the camper van, she saw several muted lights, some flashing, others steady. The systems had their own battery backups. The familiar odor of warm electronics pervaded the space, especially as she edged closer to the center of the van.

His hand was at her elbow and she met his gaze, or rather, felt herself meeting it. It was impossible to sense anything in this cramped, blacked-out space except for the latent heat of his body as it bridged the mere inches between their torsos.

Their legs, their thighs, were up against each other. She should pull back, push against his chest. But she couldn't. Not anymore. Not now, after she'd found out he was FBI. Sure, Toni would scream at her, tell her check the facts about who employed him, but it didn't matter.

She believed Jay.

Chapter 22

Hades bells. Jay prided himself on his ability to focus under the most extreme circumstances. Hell, it was why he'd been chosen for undercover work in the first place. It had to be the hit to the head that was causing him to be so distracted, so intent on proving his worth to Willow.

He took a step back, enlarging the space between them to infinitesimal.

"I'm going to look out the back window."

"No. Let me." Her hands grasped his upper arms as her breath fanned his face. The mixture of a sweet aroma from the soda and peanuts from the trail mix accentuated what had been driving him nuts since she'd walked into Veronica's office. Willow's scent. Pure feminine musk. "You're still a bit shaky." She eased past him, and he heard her slow, very quiet steps to the side of the van.

He was shaky all right, but not from the conk to his temple.

"Hang on," he whispered. "Let's make sure we're ready for bear." His fingers felt the cupboard behind him, under the propane stove, and opened it, then continued their search for the gun safe he kept hidden behind a bin of cleaning supplies, deep in the vehicle's wall. The pad lit up as soon as he touched it. He entered the sixteen-digit code and opened the safe, automatically grabbing the weapons that were already fully loaded. He'd trained for this exact situation dozens of times if not hundreds. He thanked his lucky stars for muscle memory as he stood, less dizzy, and stepped behind Willow.

"Here." He reached for her hand, gave her the weapon. "It's a Ruger .45."

"I'll take it. It's better than my backup." He heard her put her backup handgun on the banquette.

His hands moved of their own volition, one at each of her hips, the Ruger in his right, as he stood behind her. "Slow. If it's another shooter, they'll fire as soon as they see you move the shade."

He felt more than saw her look at her watch, the hands of which, like his, glowed in the dark van. "It's sunup. They won't see the shade move if we're lucky, as we're parked facing north."

If he hadn't already been impressed with Willow's astute perception, this observation would have won him over. Because their current situation of being parked in the middle of the woods on mountainous terrain at this particular time of day hadn't been part of his takedown plan, he'd never considered how the sun reflected off the van's polarized windows.

"You don't have to hang on to me, Jay. I know how to get down."

"I'm lightheaded, remember?"

"Whatever. Now, stay still."

He complied, keeping her hips under his hands. Purely as a defensive precaution.

Willow knew she became totally focused on a task to the point of being able to block out all distractions. Her colleagues had often jested that she went to another realm when tracking cybercriminals via live operations. They understood the talent as they all had it, too. It was intrinsic to being a useful cyberwarrior.

But she'd never had to work an op in the field with the man she'd found irresistible holding her hips from behind. Jay's head wound wasn't slowing him down one bit. Part of her was grateful, but another part wished he was unconscious and not providing such a potent distraction.

"Shh. I need to focus." She kept her volume low and avoided looking over her shoulder. The low morning light was creeping in through the sides of the window shades, and looking into Jay's eyes, this close, would put them both at risk.

Try flat-out dead.

Yeah, if there was another shooter out there, they were sitting ducks.

She regrouped, doing her best to ignore him, forget about the warm breath on her nape. They'd both definitely heard the crack, and two more, within the last few minutes. If someone was firing at the van, though, they would have hit it, since they weren't moving. Unless the shooter was a very bad shot, and anyone working for the Badger syndicate or Mexican cartel knew how to use a weapon.

And could she and Jay have heard something else?

Sticks breaking under a mountain bike, a heavy hiker's foot or an animal? Maybe a hunter?

There was no way to know without looking.

"What are you waiting for?" Jay's growl reverberated through her via his warm hands. Damn it.

"Shh." She reached for the blinds switch and flipped it to manual. Millimeter by millimeter she moved the lever, until the morning light, now brighter, almost blinded her. She glanced at the van's wall to allow her pupils to adjust.

"So far so good. No one shooting," she said.

"But what do you see?" Jay's impatience rasped against her last nerve.

"If you'll be quiet for a second, I'll let you know." She peered through the window, at the edge. Trees. Lots of tree trunks, and plenty of undergrowth in the form of ferns and shrubs. Two large radar dish–size objects, facing directly at her.

"We've got a male suspect, carrying two pieces of heavy armor," she said.

"What?" Jay's fingers dug into her hips as he obviously wanted to see for himself, but knew it could be a lethal mistake.

"It's two bull elks. We heard them fighting. The cracks were their antlers colliding."

She leaned back, not caring it was into Jay, allowing relief to flow over her, savoring the rich vibration of Jay's quiet laughter. As they stood there, together, their mutual relief morphed into something more tangible, insistent.

Delicious desire.

Jay couldn't have willed his erection away if he imagined Willow was an ogre. But he couldn't be with her, couldn't go further unless he knew beyond a doubt that she trusted him. Completely.

She placed her weapon on the side ledge and turned in his arms, waiting. He set his weapon down, too, but kept his arms lower, both hands loosely on her hips

"We can't do this, Wil."

"Oh, we're doing it, Jay." Her arms reached around his neck.

He groaned as he took her wrists and lowered her arms,

put a few inches between them. "You don't trust me. This can't be more than sex if that's the case, and I'm too old, this op is too far gone, the chance we could be killed—"

"Shut up, Jay." She stared at him with eyes the most beautiful shade of light brown mixed with emerald in the golden aura of morning. "We're in the middle of nowhere, our shooter died last night and there aren't any people around or even hunters. Those bull elks are prime targets. Now, we will need to move, and soon, but I'd say we have some business to attend to first, wouldn't you?" She unzipped her jacket, let it fall to the floor. "Where the heck is the bed in this van, by the way?"

"It's in the ceiling. But we're not using it until I have your word on something." He swallowed, and if he weren't so turned on, he knew his palms would be sweating bullets.

"What's that, Jay?"

"Do you believe me? That I'm a good guy?"

"Jay. I knew you were a good guy the moment I met you. But you did give me a run for a bit there, acting as dodgy as you did."

"You're not answering." He gritted his teeth against his lust. If she didn't—

"Yes, I believe you, Jay. You're FBI, and I'm a private security contractor. That makes us excellent partners. But I'm not so sure you're in the right place to make such a serious decision. Your head wound and all." Her tongue darted out as she licked her lips before her teeth caught her bottom lip.

Jay's restraint shattered.

Chapter 23

"My head's just fine, babe." A growl as his hands moved to her ass, pulled her tight against him. Shock waves of exquisite pleasure pulsed out from her deepest parts, weakening her knees.

Trepidation fought the swirls of desire in Wil's gut as she took in the intense heat in Jay's eyes—and the clear communication from his erection as it pressed against her center. She had to ignore the ugly gash she'd taped together with small butterfly bandages, had to forget that maybe Jay wasn't making the best decision with such an injury.

Wil knew there was only one thing left to do. One action she had to take, no matter the consequences.

She leaned in and pressed her lips to his, not softly or gently or with any care about his injury. Her tongue traced his lips, their salty firmness, the whiskers she'd never noticed; Jay the accountant was clean shaven. The Jay she wanted inside her, the man she'd seen through his undercover persona, had a delightfully rougher edge.

Jay groaned and his tongue met hers, drew her into his mouth with zero flirtation. If she thought he'd play possum and let her lead, she'd been mistaken. His fingers were insistent on her butt, at her waist, reaching under her T-shirt to clasp her eager breast. He backed her against the tiny kitchen counter and used his legs to spread hers apart, triggering a moan she barely recognized as her own. As their kiss deepened, their caresses became strokes to the point of frenzy. She silently damned the clothing between them to the pits of hell.

"Willow." He spoke as he dragged his mouth across her jaw, down her throat. She leaned back, exposing more for the wondrous movements of his tongue against her skin.

"Don't talk." She reached for his waist, the button at the top of his fly. As she unfastened his pants and reached inside, she felt the rock hardness of his abs, her hand then moving lower, wrapping around the equally hard length of him.

His hand captured her wrist and he pulled back from gently sucking her earlobe. "Are you sure? Because we can't go back to colleagues once we do this."

"We've never been colleagues until an hour ago. And haven't you ever heard of 'off the books'?" She gripped harder, started moving her hand. He didn't stop her, his breathing coming in gasps.

"Willow, we want this to last."

"Why? There's plenty of time before we have to be back in the office." She nipped at his jawline. "Once isn't—"

"Take your own advice, Willow." He reached behind her and must have hit a switch, because the back ceiling lowered…and became a king-size bed.

"I can't wait, Jay." She all but screamed as he palmed her breast, his forefinger and thumb holding her nipple captive.

"Enjoy, babe." He lowered his head, and his mouth replaced his fingers on her breast.

"What about you?" She gasped, tried to reach for him, but he held her wrists to the counter.

"No more talking."

* * *

Her skin was as soft as he'd imagined, more so. He wanted to savor every last bit of her. Patience had never been a virtue of his, but for Willow he'd do what he could to put off his gratification until he knew he'd completely satisfied her.

They took turns unfastening, unzipping and shimmying out of their layers of clothing until at last they were where he'd wanted to be with Willow since he'd first looked into her eyes.

Bare naked, skin to skin, alone. Together.

"Hang on." He spoke through a clenched jaw as he left her standing in the tiny galley and walked the two steps to the back of the van. "I'll get the bed. You'll find condoms in my dopp kit, in the bathroom." He quickly swept away the piles of clothing and linens that he'd stored atop the bed.

"Found it," she said. He heard her unzip the bag, the distinctive crackle of foil wrappers. When she emerged from the closet-size bathroom, she shut the door and stood with the strip of condoms hanging from her hand. "You're going to need more." Her saucy grin made his breath catch, his heartbeat pounding in his ears.

He allowed his gaze to linger on her beautiful features for a full second before he looked lower, to her full breasts, then lower, to where her waist knifed in and emphasized the remarkable curve of her hips. When his gaze got to the v of her legs he stopped, *needed* to stop, and he slapped the mattress next to him.

"Come here, Willow, unless you want this over before we get to the best part."

Her laugh danced off the small confines of the van as she made a quick jump up onto the bed, turning to face him after she landed on her side.

"Whoa, you could have hit your head on the roof." Not that he cared about the roof, or even her head at this point. Jay wasn't waiting a moment more to claim her, to do what he'd told himself he wouldn't, but had continued to fantasize about it since day one with Willow.

But as he leaned in to kiss her, he saw her wince.

"What?"

"Nothing—I twisted my ankle earlier, is all."

"You're such a damn Marine, Willow. Let me make it feel better." He spoke against her lips, his tongue dipping in and out of her mouth as she maneuvered under him. He used her shifting to raise his head and move to her belly, to the patch of hair he felt more than saw as it brushed against his face in the dark interior. He'd take his time later. Right now, he needed to make Willow feel what his body was promising him: total surrender into their hot union.

He tasted her.

"That feels…unbelievable." She spoke through gasps, her fingers grasping his hair, her hips gyrating in frenzied circles, bucking to follow his tongue. "I can't, I won't—" Her keening consumed her remaining words and he kept kissing her, loving her. Primal validation rang in his ears, of how wonderful he'd made her feel. Of what they were about to feel, together.

"I can't wait anymore, Willow."

"Then don't."

Still reeling from her most intense orgasm in a decade— *don't you mean ever?*—Willow felt around the mattress for the strip of condoms, tore one off in the dark. Their breathing sounded as if they'd finished an uphill marathon, and only added to the lusty sparks she swore she felt coursing under her skin, over every single nerve ending.

"Give it to me." His hand briefly wrapped around hers before he took the packet. The few seconds it took him to don the protection stretched as if it were an hour, but her impatience was forgotten the moment he moved back over her, placed his knees between her legs as she opened wide, her hunger for him at the starvation point.

He didn't flirt or take his time with their union. Searing heat started in her pelvis and radiated from her center as Jay thrust again and again, his raspy whispers teasing her, his whiskers against her ear. She wanted to say her own words, make him feel the intensity of the wave she rode as it crested, then broke—

"Jay!" she cried as she spasmed, her legs wrapped around him and her feet digging into his lower back. "Don't stop."

"Never." He was on his elbows, pushing into her again and again, never satisfied with one orgasm but waiting until the next wave overcame her. And the next.

Until his entire body stiffened and he shouted her name, still moving to make her climax with him.

They weren't performing no-strings sex, or engaging in a physical release after a life-threatening situation. As she floated in the dreamy post-lovemaking ambience, she acknowledged that this was what connection was all about. And maybe not a little bit of commitment.

Willow didn't want to leave this total bliss, wanted to keep experiencing the vibrant colors their lovemaking sent bursting across her closed lids. Would it be so bad to stay together like this indefinitely?

But maybe that wasn't the question she should be asking herself. Was any kind of relationship with an undercover agent ever going to be possible?

Chapter 24

It hadn't been an indefinite amount of time, but when Jay awoke with his body next to the warm curve of Willow's, the early-morning light had brightened, pouring through the window blinds they'd left half tilted after they spotted the bull elks.

Her steady breathing amazed him. Not because he was in awe of all that was Willow—but he was—but for what it signified. She'd admitted she'd believed he was part of Badger, the entire Clayton syndicate, or perhaps the Mexican cartel. Yet she lay against him, sound asleep, the Ruger he gave her on a shelf.

He felt badly about her weapon landing in the gulch, probably sitting at the bottom of the river. But he'd had no choice with that turn or how he'd taken it. He knew a Marine valued their weaponry highly. Willow was the epitome of a Marine, from how she handled her weapons to her steely composure under pressure. Which made having it ripped from her hands worse somehow.

Pride warmed his belly as he recalled handing her the weapon he knew she'd be most comfortable with on short notice. The way her gaze had met his and silently acknowledged her appreciation.

"What's so funny?" she murmured to his chest, where her face lay.

"I'm not laughing. It's just that I never thought we'd be here." Her hair tickled his nose. He buried it deeper, inhaled the scents of her shampoo and musk.

"Where, in your van?" She went to sit up, and he tightened his arm around her shoulder. "Or post–hooking up?"

"Easy, babe. The roof is closer than you think in here."

"Right. I'm not the one with the bump on my head, though. How's the cut?" She settled back down next to him, her head on his chest.

"It's letting me know it's there, but I'll live." He moved his fingers in circles around her shoulder, the smooth skin a miracle of nature. "I know your brain is already ten steps ahead. What are you thinking?"

"That I'd happily stay in all day with you. If we could call in—wait, what time is it?" She shifted and held her arm up in front of her face. "We have to be at the office soon, Jay."

"At least it's Sunday morning. Veronica starts three hours later, so the staff does, too. It's a skeleton staff for the most part, save for me, Derek and Veronica."

"Great, so we have time to grab a shower before we report." She revealed a saucy smile.

"We?" He shook his head. "It's time for you to step back. I have to finish this. You'll be a risk I can't afford. And it's not just me, it's my entire team, right down to the newbie analysts working nonstop at bureau headquarters."

"Hang on." She put her finger over his lips and he mock bit it. "Let's keep it simple. We'll go into work as scheduled. You have to admit, it'll be interesting to see Veronica and Derek's reactions to us still being alive. If they're surprised, we know they ordered the hit, which they would only do if they've figured out your real identity. My death would be no more than collateral damage to them. If not—"

"We're looking at the Mexican cartel, or one of any other factions within the two. It's a lot more complicated than what you might have found out from your mother's sources, Wil."

"I figured as much," she said. They lay in silence, lost in their individual thoughts, but together in a way he couldn't articulate if asked. One thing he knew for certain, though: He didn't want to talk about work. Not yet.

"You know, the first time or two I stayed in here, I banged my head but good on the air conditioner." He pointed at the square vent above their heads.

"Ah, change of subject. I'm game." She pointedly looked at the AC unit. "I'm surprised you equipped this van with AC, or didn't take it out for the PNW." The PNW usually suffered through two to three weeks of hot summer weather annually, tops. "You could have used the space for another battery, or a system server." Her cajoling tone revealed that while she'd trusted him to make love to her, she might not trust him completely. She was more comfortable with their banter. Wil gently prodded him as she sat up again. "What were you thinking?"

"Hey." He reached for her, not caring an iota about his van's configuration. All he knew was that he couldn't let this time together end. Willow couldn't leave his side. Not yet.

To his delighted surprise, instead of sliding off the platform bed, she moved atop him, careful to keep her head low and away from the protruding AC. She placed her hands on his shoulders and he reveled in taking her weight as she leaned in close, her mouth a whisper above his.

"Hey, what?" She kissed him, fully and sexily. "Wait— don't tell me. Let me guess." She kissed his nose. "You want a replay of the last few hours?" She kissed his chin, his jaw.

"Or you want to run away to Mexico together? Long days on the beach, longer nights in bed?"

"Hawaii would be good about now, too. The main island. No pesky tourists." He could get used to lying here, soaking up her attention.

So could his erection, which the raise of her brow let him know she was very aware of. "Is this just your usual morning—"

"It's all you, Willow." He pulled her fully down on top of him, ending their conversation.

"We need to go back to the house, act as if nothing has happened. And we need to be careful. I don't know if the motorcycle shooter was the same person I chased away from the house two nights ago or not." She was dressed, and turned away while Jay dressed. He'd refused her help and insisted his balance was back, that a small headache was all that remained from his injury.

"I'm not disagreeing with you about keeping things as normal, hell, it was my idea. But you'll never convince me that you need to return to Mack as my bodyguard. This isn't like anything you've experienced in combat, or behind a computer."

Ouch.

This was the problem with allowing herself to be vulnerable, to giving in to her physical needs. It left her wide-open for a zinger, for Jay to stop her from doing what she planned.

"It's not all about you or your supposed takedown." She opened the door and stepped out into the woods, needing space from him. A sharp crack sounded and she froze before remembering the elk. Looking to her right, she met the angry gaze of the larger bull from earlier. His breath formed large white puffs and he grunted. "You don't have to tell me twice, buddy." Willow went back into the van.

"Um, we definitely need to drive out of here if at all possible. Eddie Elk isn't going to let us hike."

"You're right about one thing. We'll go back to the campsite, provided the van cooperates." He strode to the front of the vehicle, as much as the cramped space allowed. "Buckle up."

She was already in the passenger seat, removing the extra shades. "I don't need you ordering me around, Jay. Great sex doesn't equal me being subservient to you."

"Whoa." He turned the driver's seat back to forward facing and sat in it, albeit gingerly. She knew he was lying about how much his head was bothering him. "You don't really believe I took advantage of you? We have something here, Wil." His use of her preferred name by anyone but family drove a nail into her heart. She loved how he said 'Willow.' *It has to be this way or you can't do your job.*

"We had a night, Jay. An early morning, actually. Let's keep it professional from here on out, okay?"

"I don't think that's possible. Look, we have to be on the same page here." He raised his hand to rake his fingers through his hair and winced.

"I agree. Which means you let me drive."

He met her gaze and she steeled herself, forced her Marine training to rescue her from the emotions that wanted to be everything to Jay. She couldn't. No one could. Jay lived for his work.

"Fine. You drive. We'll figure out what you can do to stay out of my way before we get into the office." He got up, and she slipped into the driver's seat and turned on the engine.

"Get buckled, Jay."

Chapter 25

They got the van moving and retraced the route back to the clearing without any issues. It was remarkable to Wil that they'd driven less than a mile last night to evade the shooter, when the entire episode replayed on a continuous loop in her mind. She was familiar with this, the aftereffects of a traumatic incident. They'd both survived, but a soul had been lost nonetheless. Wil would have preferred to capture the motorcycle rider, to bring them to justice. And to get some intel out of them, information that might help Jay.

Correction: She wanted intel that she could pass to Toni, who'd send it to the appropriate authorities. She had to keep her priorities straight—sexy times with Jay had to remain a one-off.

For now.

She mentally brushed away the thought as they hiked back to the house. As soon as she heard Jay finish his shower—she'd reminded him to keep his wound dry— she took a quick one, never forgetting that she was still his bodyguard, whether an FBI agent needed one or not. With a towel still wrapped around her head, she pulled out her laptop. Within thirty seconds she was talking to Toni via video chat. A minute later, she'd recounted the entire evening and early morning to Toni. Not mentioning the sex she'd mistaken for lovemaking, of course.

"You've got to be kidding me, Willow." Toni's expression said more than her words. "You should have let me know your status as soon as you two stopped the van. As soon as any shots were fired, to be fair."

"I couldn't."

"Didn't you have your comms set up to our feed?" Toni's eyes narrowed, and Willow heard her fingers typing. "Ah, that's a big negative." A thunderous expression replaced Toni's initial relief that Wil was okay, as well as Jay. "What were you thinking?"

"I was thinking that I had to keep us both alive, Toni. And you're right, I should have checked in sooner. At least about the dead shooter."

"We can't be certain he's dead until we get a police report saying as much, if anyone ever finds him, in fact," Toni said.

"You will. The cliff over the river is at least two hundred feet tall. No one survives that."

"Maybe not." Toni stared into her camera. "What now, sister? Tell me what you're thinking, because you're sure as heck not following my directions."

"That's not fair. I'm doing absolutely everything we agreed upon. So I was a little late reporting in—you had nothing to worry about."

"Go on." Toni sipped from a mug imprinted with Sisters Are Forever. Willow knew this because it had been one of her and Aubrey's gift to Toni on her fortieth birthday. "Amuse me."

"Stop being so dramatic, will you? Nothing's changed. Jay and I are going back in to Mack as if nothing happened." She explained her motives for this. "I promise I'll let you know immediately if I think Veronica Clayton was behind the hit."

"That's not going to tell us a heck of a lot, frankly. But as you know, every little bit helps." Toni sighed. "I'm wondering if maybe I was wrong, sis."

"How so?"

"In keeping you there. We do our job and serve the public whenever we can. We even have our own agents working undercover alongside LE, as you know. But this isn't the same. You were hired for personal protection, period. You haven't had any of the advanced undercover training I send our select agents to—who, by the way, have all worked in undercover roles before we hired them. You haven't."

She straightened, allowed her resolve to fuel her argument. Toni was a formidable foe when she wanted to be. The quintessential big sister, except now she held authority over Willow's career choices.

This feels a lot more like a life choice.

"No, but I'm acting as a bodyguard, which, in truth, is what I'm doing here. Along with keeping my ear to the ground and finding out more about Mack, the Claytons and their relationship to Badger."

"There are two things you need to know, Willow. First, accept the fact that the Clayton syndicate *is* Badger. As of last night, Veronica Clayton took over three smaller, local rings. But very awful rings, because two are involved in crack manufacturing and distribution, and the other conducts human trafficking, providing underage girls and boys to local prostitution rings."

Her stomach churned in revulsion but her desire to help bring any of these bad players to justice prevailed. "What's the second piece of information?"

"It's actually not about Badger or the Mexican cartel, directly. It's about Veronica Clayton, who was Veronica Miller before she married Cal." Toni paused, made sure Willow was looking into her camera. "Her real name is Veronica Adams." Toni paused and something in her expression made Wil sit up straighter. "So...?"

"Adams is a common name, but in this instance, it's not. I mean, it's related to the case you're working on, Wil."

"Wait a damn minute. Adams as in Sarah Adams?" Incredulity slammed into her composure. "She's related to one of the girls in my cold case?"

"Yes. Sarah Adams was Veronica's older sister." Toni said.

"Do you know why she changed her name, went by an alias?"

Toni's fingers were making the clacking noise on her favored mechanical keyboard. She claimed it helped her think better. "Yes, let's see. According to a social and family services report filed thirty years ago, both Veronica and her brother, Sam, were removed from their family within weeks of the disappearance of Sarah and the other two girls. She never had a father, not living with her, and her mother was charged with negligence. Her mother surrendered her rights and stayed in town to perform community service, after which she, for all practical purposes, also disappeared."

"Charming." Willow's frustration had to be shelved. She wouldn't be able to process this vital information fully, or use it toward solving the cold case, until after the looming takedown was over. "It doesn't explain why Veronica went to the dark side, though."

"I'm sure you'll figure that out, sis." Toni's focus was back on Willow. "I know I can't convince you to quit, and I'm as committed to seeing Badger disbanded as you now are. It will also be a great feather in Cascade Confidential's hat. But you're my sister, and I'll never forgive myself if anything happens to you. Nothing is worth losing you, sis."

"You're not going to lose me."

"Promise you'll pull out if your internal red flags pop up?"

"Promise."

"I don't suppose you're going to tell me how hot the sex was with Jay, are you?"

"Wha—"

"These new laptop cameras are so clear. I can make out everything on your skin, sister." Toni grinned. "Keep me up-to-date, and no delays this time." Toni's image disappeared.

Willow darted to the bathroom mirror, and saw what Toni had. A love bite, on the front of her neck. It could pass as a bruise, she supposed, but she hadn't fooled Toni.

"It's a hickey," she whispered to herself. No love involved.

Chapter 26

Jay wondered if the ugly truth was what was keeping Willow as uncommunicative as him, and immediately chastised himself for focusing on anything besides his job. Since agreeing to forget that they'd had their intimate interlude—since when had he ever called a good roll in bed that?—for the sake of saving lives and bringing the entire Badger syndicate to justice, they'd not exchanged any significant words.

"Same place, same outward appearance." She spoke quietly as she wiped her mouth, half of her breakfast burrito still in the container on her lap. They were back in her company SUV, parked on a Pine Hills side street, out of view of the main highway.

"It's not too late to bail, you know." He had to offer her an out. Because if things went south, he had to know it had been her decision. The weight of Willow's life on his shoulders was too much to ever bear. Accepting that their lovemaking was, in fact, a hookup, a one-off, was hard enough.

She gave him a scathing glance. "If I thought for one second that I was jeopardizing your hard-won inroads, trust me. I would bail. Which means I'm right where I need to be, and in turn, that means that you have to trust me. You know I can do my job, right?"

"Of course." He wasn't giving her lip service. Willow was just as proficient as any other agent he'd worked with. He'd never admit it to his partner—or Willow, of course. "This isn't about trust anymore, though. It's about knowing that we have no control over Veronica's next moves." He bit his tongue to keep from calling her *Willow*. Logic demanded that he stop thinking of her as anything more than a colleague. For both their sakes. He had to keep calling her Wil, period. And better if he could get himself to think of her as Wil. Not the Willow he'd made passionate love to...

Not everything in life can be compartmentalized.

He ignored the voice of his conscience. Whatever this was between him and Willow, it had nothing to do with logic or common sense. He'd felt something bigger, more significant, with her. The hot sex was a welcome benefit, but it was the frosting to the irresistible woman he wished he'd met sooner in life. Before he'd committed to his undercover lifestyle.

Doing his job as an agent was the only way to move forward. Which meant letting go of any fantasy that Willow had made him a different man, one who was capable of settling down in one place under his real name.

"While we still have a few minutes alone, tell me what I can do to best help you accomplish your mission." She'd read his mind.

The Willow he'd come to know at work was back in full force. As if last night hadn't happened. As if they hadn't almost both lost everything, then tasted what *everything* could mean for them. He pushed aside the disconcerting thought and faced her, intending to give her definite ground rules to adhere to.

Bad idea. Looking at Willow when they were alone and she was within reach was never a smart move. Sure, he'd made up his mind that he had no future with any woman, but it didn't stop his body from reacting.

Her long hair was pulled back in that too-perfect ponytail, and her minimal makeup said "boss lady" more than "sex kitten," but he couldn't stop visualizing how she'd looked in the throes of her orgasms. How her insides had gripped his hardness. Worse, how her pleasure had triggered a rush of passion, joy and ecstasy he'd never had with another woman.

"Well?" An arched brow accompanied her prompt. Willow was over it—best he follow suit.

He inhaled, looked through the windshield at two squirrels chasing each other, one with a huge chestnut in its mouth. On an exhale, he faced her with resolve.

"At the risk of irritating you, I'm going to repeat my needs. What I really need, what my job requires most, is for you to get out of this situation before it gets too hot. But you've repeatedly refused to cooperate, so fine. You're along for the ride. But it's my ride. My team's calling the shots, Wil, which means you do what I tell you to. It's not a power struggle unless you make it one." He didn't have to say more. She knew as well as he did that one call to his superior would force Cascade Confidential to pull her out. He'd let Janice know that he'd revealed his identity to her, and typical for Janice, she'd not reacted except to remark "you know best."

"I get it." He didn't have to look over at her to know her chin jutted out in that maddening way. He had her over a barrel.

"Right. So all you have to do is play the part you've been doing, as my bodyguard. For today. Maybe tomorrow. It's a good idea that you had, actually, for us to see what Veronica and Derek's reactions will be, if any, when we show up. But know that if it goes down while you're still at Mack, you stand back, stay out of harm's way. You don't even attempt to stop my actions, no matter how illogical they may look to you."

"Fine. But will you at least tell me where you've stashed your own weapons? Are they in the main building or one of the warehouses?"

A laugh escaped him. "Forgive me if I forget that you have some of the same training as me."

"Probably more." She didn't sound annoyed, or uppity. They were back to their banter. He let out a long sigh. This was good, being professional partners. They were good together.

Professionally.

"Maybe. I have half a dozen handguns and two grenades in a lockbox inside my locker in the rec center." He gave her the code, not doubting that she'd commit it to memory.

She coughed on her latte. "Grenades? You're not messing around."

"Neither are Badger or the Claytons."

"No." Hesitation flitted across her expression. "My sister—my boss, Toni—she filled me in on what Badger and its newest acquisitions are capable of. What they've done."

"Right. So no need to go over that. We both need to be as clear minded as we can. The other thing I need from you is to tell me at once if you see or suspect anything suspicious."

"Now you do sound like my boss."

"Better than sounding like your sister." He got a tiny lift of the corner of her mouth at his last.

He knew without question that Willow would be able to handle herself in the unlikely event of a firefight. He hoped to see Veronica and Derek, and their posse, in cuffs before it came to that. Except… "Look, we don't know who our assailant was last night, if he's still alive. There's a chance he told Veronica what happened. Then we're sitting ducks walking into the building."

"We can be reasonably assured he's dead," she said. "I told Toni, no one survives a two-hundred-foot drop."

"I want to agree with you, but since it hasn't been on the local news or police scanner, and we didn't go back and investigate the scene, we can't rule out that whoever it was has let their contacts know that we engaged them. I need to go in there alone, Wil."

His words sounded nuts even to him, which meant only one thing. He was too wrapped up in keeping Willow safe.

He'd just found her, discovered a piece of himself he'd long buried. The caring, human part. A future with her, with any woman, was out of the question. But his dedication to duty wasn't.

He wasn't going to risk Willow's life.

"You're going back to Mack alone over my dead body." As Willow spoke to him her hands itched to grab Jay's now clean-shaven face and turn it toward her, so that she could look into his eyes. But he'd drawn the blackout shades on his interior motives. "Your reasoning makes zero sense. Let's say our motorcycle dude worked for Veronica. Or he was an extra hire by Derek, who we both know is suspicious of both of us. He likes to keep things nice and tight between him and Veronica, am I right?"

She didn't wait for him to respond but pressed on. "Presuming the bike guy is dead, the syndicate hasn't heard a peep from him since last night. We have to go in there like we planned, as if nothing happened. I don't show up by your side, protecting you, trust me, Veronica or Derek are going to know something has changed. They might think I got killed."

He rubbed the back of his neck. "Yeah, probably."

"The way I see it, we play it cool as cucumbers." She winced at her simile, because the long, hard vegetable only made her think of what pure ecstasy she'd enjoyed thanks to Jay's cu—

"Can you do that? Can you not give Veronica one of your looks?" He looked at her, and his entire countenance had gone taut, grave. "She's the epitome of evil, and you can't underestimate her intelligence. Sure, you've seen more in your military service than she can imagine, but it won't matter if you're captured by her thugs and she orders them to slit your throat."

"But not before they torture, probably rape me, just for her sick kicks, right?" Willow's gut twisted in revulsion at the acts she enumerated, but she had to make Jay see that she knew the risks, knew what she was getting into. She wasn't going to leave him to finish this alone.

"Yes."

"You have an entire team waiting to come in as soon as you have proof or a signal that she's giving herself away, don't you? I can keep myself alive until SWAT or whoever else you have lined up arrives, Jay."

"There's no wiggle room with you, is there?" he said.

"Nope." She turned away, restarted the vehicle and cracked her window in an effort to clear the side windows, which were fogging up from their conversation. And she couldn't help but wish the steamy windows were due to her and Jay doing some wiggling.

Mission first.

Chapter 27

They walked together into a rather subdued atmosphere at Mack headquarters, which she expected since it was late Sunday morning. Anything would seem quiet, boring even, after the twelve hours she'd just had with Jay, but their entrance was definitely anticlimactic. Derek offered a brief nod as he strode out of Veronica's office, headed for his own.

No sign of him being aware of what they'd been through last night.

"You look too relaxed," Jay said under his breath as they settled into his cubicle. "You need more of your over-the-top professionalism back in play. And some makeup over that hickey."

Her cheeks heated and she was careful to not make eye contact, choosing instead to focus on his display screens as he powered on the Mack computers. Her fingers quickly buttoned her top buttons, and she had to hope the collar would work like a turtleneck did in high school.

Jay was right; as they'd discussed over the last of their breakfast in the car, it was imperative that they keep up their appearance of barely putting up with one another. It sure didn't seem to be a stretch for Jay.

You can do this.

No matter where she'd served around the world, or whom she stood next to, whom she'd made love to the night before, Wil had never brought her personal emotions and experiences along with her in uniform. No matter that her Marine uniform had been traded for comfortable black dress pants, a tailored white shirt and dark leather jacket. A job was a job, and her job wasn't to mentally relive the ecstasy she'd enjoyed at Jay's fingertips. That would wait until after.

After what? After this assignment ended in either a firefight or the anticlimactic apprehension of Veronica Clayton, Derek Michaels and their cronies?

She was making too much of this.

Are you, though? As she watched Jay settle into his chair—because that's what a good security detail would do—her gaze lingered on the too-large work shirt, his ugly tie, the high-waisted dress pants secured with a worn belt that boasted a hand-tooled belt buckle right out of a rodeo. She peered closer.

Numbers Dude.

The belt buckle wasn't of a cowboy on a bucking bronco as she'd first thought, but of the Wall Street bull, the wording above it.

"See something interesting, Miss Marine?" Derek had walked up to the cubicle and wore his usual crap-eating grin. Her gut twisted and her fist closed. No one denigrated the Marine Corps.

"It's Wil." She fought to keep her polite smile.

"Whatever." He turned his back on her and effectively blocked her view of Jay. "J-man, the boss needs to see you now."

"I don't have the morning reports done yet. I need ten more minutes," Jay said. As Willow observed, Derek continued to stare at Jay, but Jay was an expert at ignoring Derek, or at least appearing to not care about the kiss-ass. This was another thing different about the civilian world from the military. Wil couldn't think of a time when she'd ignored a superior's request. Although Derek wasn't really Jay's boss. More like his babysitter.

And yet Veronica Clayton had hired her to protect Jay. That told her everything she needed to know about Derek's capabilities.

"You seem to forget who works for who, buddy." Derek was also very big on pecking order, something that would be left unsaid if he was secure in his position.

"I work for Veronica, and she trusts me to provide her with the latest and greatest financial picture." Jay's fingers flew over his keyboard, and the clicking of the keys drowned out Derek's grumble as he turned and walked away.

Wil's gut felt like a thousand tiny porcupines were rubbing against it—the wrong way.

"Don't you think you should be a bit nicer?" she whispered.

"Not at all." He paused, cast her a piercing glance. Sure, he still looked like the nerdy accountant he portrayed, but in the depths of his gaze, the shimmer of the keen intelligence it took to conduct a complex op like this was clear. As was his irritation with her.

"I'm the one calling the shots here. Don't forget it." He turned back to his computer. As if they were no more than work colleagues.

As much as it stung, she needed the reminder that while they'd made a perfect pair in bed, Jay wasn't thinking about that now. She shouldn't be, either. Her primary job remained, no matter how much their sexy times had thrown her emotions off-kilter. Wil had to keep Jay alive, period.

She'd sort out her heart's status later.

* * *

Jay wished to hell and back that he'd insisted Willow return to wherever her office was in Coeur d'Alene. She could have made up whatever excuses necessary, and how hard would have it been for her boss, her sister, Toni, to tell Veronica Clayton that she had a replacement on the way, but delay indefinitely? His team had assured him they had contacted local LE as well as CC to ensure all players were who they said they were. Both CC and Willow had been thoroughly vetted, beyond the initial research by Janice. And much to his consternation, everyone from his boss to the newest team analyst supported Willow's presence by his side. He had to admit, it gave him a level of comfort that his cover hadn't been blown, something he would have thought more possible if he'd come back to Mack alone this morning.

Derek had taken the hint to buzz off, but he knew it was temporary. When the lackey returned, Jay knew he'd better have his report in hand, ready to present to Veronica. Without acting any differently than he had his entire time as Mack's CPA. His phone buzzed, the new burner he'd initialized this morning after his shower. He pulled it out of his pants pocket and looked at the screen.

DAFFODIL

It was his team's code word indicating that the Badger syndicate was about to take action. The intel analysts had gotten wind, or definite facts, that Veronica was about to claim her perceived chair as CEO of all things wrong about the world.

Which, judging from the sight of Derek stalking back

to his cubicle with his mouth set in a grim line, was about to get more interesting.

"You're up, J-man." Derek looked at Willow. "You stay here, Chesty. Get it? Chesty Puller was a famous Marine. I just read about him on the internet. I should have thought of it sooner—it's a perfect nickname for you." His gaze pointedly dropped to Willow's chest. Jay's composure was hard-won, as his shoulder ached with the right hook he'd have loved to plant in Derek's smirk.

"My name is Wil." Ice shards hung from each word she spoke. "General Puller was the most highly decorated Marine, ever. His name isn't to be denigrated. By anyone."

"Whoa, sorry there, sparky." Derek held his hands up in mock surrender. "Take it easy. I was just pulling your leg."

If he wasn't so keen on keeping it together and not punching Derek's lights out, Jay would have laughed. He was pretty certain Willow's stellar professionalism was the only thing holding her back from giving Derek the verbal lashing he deserved.

"Okay, then, *Wil*." Derek's lips curled into a sneer.

Patience.

Patience was the ally of a successful covert operation. Always.

Jay gathered up the printed materials Veronica insisted on—she wasn't as tech savvy as she wanted everyone to believe—and stood, sparing Willow a quick glance. It was enough to confirm she had the same thoughts about Derek as he did.

"I promise I'll come right back." Said for Derek's benefit, but damn if he didn't wish it were true. That he could promise Willow the world, in fact.

Her eyes widened infinitesimally, a quick spark—of interest, anger, hope?—and then her shutters were sealed up again, tight. Nothing Derek would notice, but it was like a kick to Jay's gut. He was definitely hyped up about the takedown to come.

Or maybe it's more to do with wanting Willow?

"Copy that. I'll be here when you get back." She had a bored expression in place, and for the second time he thought she'd be excellent at undercover work. Which, according to the Cascade Confidential profile that Janice had sent him, was something they did now and again, for preferred clients.

"Okay, let's do it." He nodded at Derek as if he believed they were really a team. As if he'd drunk the Clayton criminal dynasty's artificially dyed and sweetened punch.

Wil's gut churned. It went against every bit of her training to remain in the cubicle while the person she was supposed to protect went out of her line of sight. But she had to make Derek believe she was no more than a rent-a-cop. Someone willing to comply with Mack's obscure security policies. A Marine who wouldn't rip Derek's jerk head off for slandering the icon of all the Marine Corps stood for. *As if.*

She knew Jay, knew he could handle himself. The Badger syndicate was bigger than Jay, though. Bigger than both of them. Not to mention the Mexican cartel and however many other gangs that Veronica planned to take down in her quest to be the Pacific Northwest kingpin.

More like queenpin.

She waited for fifteen seconds after Jay and Derek had disappeared around the corner. Then she made her move.

Chapter 28

"This is all fine." Veronica waved her hand over the spreadsheets he'd printed. She hadn't made a pretense of scanning the numbers, which Jay found telling. Veronica was distracted.

She's getting ready to make her move, all right.

As he stood in front of her desk, she threw him a glare. "Sit down, Jay. You're making me nervous." Another tell. Veronica never admitted to weakness of any kind, and her tone hadn't reflected sarcasm. His nape prickled and he braced himself for whatever was to come.

As he sat down, Derek remained standing behind him, out of his peripheral vision. *Not ideal.* He knew the man was still in the CEO's office by his unmistakable heavy breathing, the squish of his soft-soled shoes as he shifted his weight. At least he didn't have to smell Derek's breath as he did in the cubicle. The man was a mouth breather, and Jay had put up with his gross coffee–and–vape pen breath since the day he'd reported here.

"Listen, Jay, I have some questions about my accounts." Interesting that Veronica referred to the Mack money as hers, and not in the collective *our.* "We need to make sure that, as a company, only I have access to them. Can you make that happen?"

"Whoa. I'm just an accountant, your numbers guy. You

need to run this past your legal team, and then I'm pretty sure you need the board of directors to agree, right?" Playing ignorant was his best defense and stall technique. He wasn't leaving this office until he knew what she was planning to do, and when.

"They've all…left." Her gaze was neutral, but her hands tightened on the edges of her glass-top desk. Her knuckles were bone white, and she hadn't so much as offered one of her fake smiles since he'd walked in here. Had she eliminated the entire board? He thought of all the people she'd already ordered the kill for, the countless victims of the drugs Badger so adeptly trafficked.

You're staring at a killer. Was he her next target? After he took care of whatever she wanted him to with the accounts access?

The tingling on Jay's nape tripped the warning bells in his mind, made his gut tense. He didn't have to wait long for physical confirmation of his internal warning signals as Veronica gave an almost imperceptible nod to his right, toward Derek.

"I'm sorry to hear that, Veronica. What about your—" He turned to look at Derek, and only then saw the jerk looming over him. Nothing out of the ordinary, except Derek's arm was up as if he were about to punch Jay. No big deal, as Jay would have this motherfudger on the ground in one move. But the object Derek held in his hand was a different matter.

A syringe.

"Get him!" Veronica's shout sounded as Derek jabbed at Jay's neck.

Wil sat in the outer office, a wall separating her from Jay in Veronica's suite. The cold steel of a ridiculously contemporary chair sliced through her slacks. She'd prefer to be leaning up against the closed door, listening to the meeting as best she could, but she had to play it cool in case another employee walked into the corporate suite. Her clothing was damp from running across the parking lot to the gym, and back again, taking advantage of her faux rapport with the security guard to get into the building without going through the metal detector, claiming she was "late for a meeting in the corporate office." He'd been in a hurry to take a smoke break, so luck was on her side.

Now she waited, carrying no fewer than four handguns and a Taser, all concealed under her clothing. Her readiness to protect Jay was incongruous to the upscale design of this outer office, replete with chrome and glass. Veronica Clayton had turned the office decor of what Wil assumed had been a bastion of testosterone under Cal Clayton's thumb into an ode to greed, providing herself with accoutrements normally associated with a Fortune 500 company that dealt in cosmetics, not timber. And whatever else the syndicate dealt in. Weapons, drugs and the worst—humans.

Her phone vibrated with a text from Toni.

I NEED REGULAR REPORTS, SIS

She quickly pecked her reply.

NTR. YET.

Nothing to report, not yet. But as she hit the send button, a shout and several loud thumps sounded on the other side of the wall. Followed by a definitive *crash*.

Wil jumped up, ran to the outer door of the suite and shut it, shoved the ugly chair up under the lever knob. It was all she had in the moment, and it would at least slow down the security guard. If he was even back at his station.

Swirling around, she faced the door into Veronica's inner sanctum. Time to bust down a door.

Grabbing her weapon from its holster, she held it in front of her and approached the entryway. She tried the doorknob. Locked. She lifted her knee and kicked against the door, hard, with as much force as she had.

Except when she fired her kick, the door burst open. Her momentum propelled her forward, right on top of the person who'd opened the door.

"Get off of me, you bitch!" Veronica Clayton wasn't aware that misogynistic epithets weren't going to get her anywhere with Wil, who easily pinned the woman down while keeping her weapon steady and ready to fire as needed.

Wil took in the scene in a split second. Derek lay with his eyes closed on the carpet to her right. Jay was behind Veronica's desk, pulling and dumping drawers from the credenza against the wall.

"Keep her down, Wil." He didn't have to say more. Wil had trained countless times on disengaging the enemy. No question, Veronica Clayton was definitely the enemy.

"You'll regret this." Veronica spat at Wil, who reared back only slightly.

"I'll never regret doing what's right." Wil kept her weapon trained on Veronica for extra measure, but it wasn't necessary. The woman looked to be in top physical condition, but it had to be the smoke-and-mirrors effect of designer clothing and plastic surgery, because the body under Wil was…frail. Pathetically so.

"What are you looking for?" Impatience tugged at her focus. "I can call 9-1-1."

"No," Jay ordered as he pulled out Veronica's high-end

handbag—Wil knew it to be worth at least two months' salary—and shook the contents onto the desk. *Pling pling pling.* Lipstick, compact mirror, wallet. *Clang.* And a set of keys, which Jay grabbed.

"Let's go." Jay headed for the door.

"You'll never find what you're looking for," Veronica snarled, still under Wil's control.

"Already did." He looked at Wil. "We're taking her with us."

How she'd gone from a simple bodyguard contract to basically kidnapping a very bad player that she really had no proof was running a syndicate was something Wil would figure out in the after times. That's what she thought of as the period when a mission, or in this case, a contract, was completed, fulfilled. She'd replay every minute of her time since the first phone call from Toni telling her to leave Coeur d'Alene right through to…what? She had no idea what the ending of this would be. Right now it looked pretty incredulous.

"I need you to let me drive. Trust me." His steely gaze met hers and for once she didn't fight him. Her job was clear: support Jay, CC's client, and hopefully glean intel she could pass to Toni.

Don't forget the cold case.

She sat in the back of the fully armored SUV with Veronica strapped in next to her, her hands and feet secured with zip ties that were part of the Cascade Confidential security kit. The plastic strips were overly large on the bone-thin woman's frame, and definitely not in the same league as Veronica's bloodred designer suit and red-soled, four-inch pumps.

Not for the first time Wil marveled at the various contracts her mother, ergo Cascade Confidential, must have accepted in order to make zip ties a standard-issue item for all CC field agents. She lifted her gaze to the profile of the woman who was not only the current kingpin of Badger but the sister of one of the Hartford girls, who'd disappeared near the Hartford mining shaft decades ago. The words fought to come out, the questions only Veronica could answer about such a dark time, but not yet. First, Jay had to do whatever he needed to strip Badger down to nothing.

She couldn't see the back of his head through the headrest as he drove with expert speed and ease, but every now and then their gazes met in the rearview mirror. Did he see her commitment to his mission reflected in her eyes?

He still hadn't revealed where they were headed. Wil hoped that this wasn't a last-minute decision on his part. FBI agents were known to plan out every detail of an op, weren't they? He had suffered a pretty hard conk to his head, and he had to have some emotional fallout from their coming together, then realizing it had been a mistake, didn't he?

Don't go there. She refocused on the present, reviewed each weapon in her possession, thought about what she should tell Toni.

CAN'T TALK. DO NOT CALL. IN SUV, JAY DRIVING, HAVE VERONICA WITH US. She quickly hit send. Toni's reply was immediate.

I HAVE YOU ON THE GPS APP. LOOKS LIKE YOU'RE HEADED TO THE CLAYTON ESTATE. ANY IDEA WHY?

Her reply was simple.

NO.

"I'm going to see both of you rot in prison for this." Veronica hadn't stopped issuing threats from the moment

Wil had tackled her. They'd left Derek in a locked office, thanks to Veronica's full set of keys. The woman proved yet again that she might have extraordinary criminal intelligence, but when it came to common sense, not so much. Who kept all of their most important keys and fobs on the same ring, when they provided access to her literal kingdom? Jay had opened the office safe and withdrawn several burner phones, handheld weapons of various makes and calibers, and something that had given him pause. She'd watched him open the ubiquitous manila file folder and give a quick nod of satisfaction. Whatever was in the folder that now rested on the SUV's passenger seat had given Jay the confidence to get them out of the building via the secret back room and on their way.

If they were going to the Clayton mansion, it had to be to talk to Cal Clayton. But wasn't he in a coma? Impatience threatened to undo Wil's composure, but she stifled it. Jay was in the lead seat.

Trust and apprehension could coexist, she realized.

Derek came to with a pounding headache. He lay on the small cot Veronica had insisted they place in the safe room. Where had he gone wrong? He always listened to Veronica, and this was where he ended up?

Flashes of how he'd ended up here came rushing back. He'd brought the numbers man into the front office, at Veronica's request. Jay had been ready to give his daily report. He'd had the syringe ready to go, and almost got him, too. Veronica pulled out her handgun, the one she carried in her purse, and aimed it at Jay. Somehow the bastard had knocked him out and kept from being shot.

Why the hell hadn't Veronica kept to their plan? They were so close. So close to the life they'd built together, with no financial worries ever again, no one to answer to, because they were in charge of the world.

But finding out the killer he'd hired had been found dead at the bottom of a canyon had spooked her. He'd only told her after the fact, because Veronica's focus had to stay on the takeover.

Veronica was prone to her moods, as he liked to think of them, but he'd always been able to calm her down. Usually with a round of rough sex, the kind they both favored. But she hadn't given any indication of being restless this morning; in fact, she'd seemed more focused than ever as she'd read her usual reports from the various departments—HR, operations, administration. She was particularly concerned with the report from security that indicated a hooded figure clad in all black had prowled about their warehouse on the north end of the property last night. The security chief had dismissed it as "some strung-out teen, looking for a quick way to make cash," and Derek concurred. Veronica hadn't been convinced, he could tell by the way the lines over her nose deepened—she was nearing her maintenance wrinkle injections—but she hadn't said anything. Murmured that she had "bigger fish to fry this morning."

And then she'd told him that her sources had informed her that Jay wasn't the man they thought he was. She didn't think he was law enforcement, but a mole for the Mexican cartel. She'd told Derek to get Jay in the office and handed him what looked like a syringe for a horse, not a human. Her only words had been "hit him with this in his neck as soon as I give you the signal."

His head continued to clear, and he looked around their safe room, which was no longer safe as far as he was concerned. There had to be scissors here somewhere.

No matter if he didn't find the scissors, he'd still escape. Because there wasn't only one way out of this room.

He'd bet that rat Jay—was that his real name?—hadn't made it far with Veronica. She'd rake that jerk over the coals, cut off his balls by the time she was done with him. Where would she go, though?

The Clayton estate.

He was sharp, even after having his lights punched out by the nerd. Veronica had told him they'd need to make one stop before she took down the Mexican cartel. She needed the list of overseas accounts she'd had their cyber geek hack from the rival syndicate. Not trusting computers, Veronica had taken the printed list and stored it in the safest place she had.

The basement vault in the Clayton mansion. He'd seen it only once, when Veronica wanted a kinkier time, in the cellar that looked like a European catacomb. The stealth safe was in its own vault, which lowered over fifty feet into the ground. He figured the industrial safe had cost close to a million to install, and now it held the account numbers, passwords and PINs for over three billion dollars. Money still made the world go round, and his and Veronica's world was about to get bigger.

He cursed the assassin he'd hired to take out Jay, and maybe even that stupid bodyguard Wil who Veronica had insisted upon until she was firmly in place as kingpin. Once he was out of here, Derek would go to the estate, meet back up with Veronica. And kill the traitor who'd betrayed them both.

First, he had to figure out how to get out of these plastic cuffs.

Chapter 29

The drive through the mountains was winding, and all three of them had grown silent. Veronica had sunk into a sulking huddle against the back passenger door. Wil was grateful for the reprieve and used the quiet to process what was going on. They'd taken a person against her will, but since Jay had incriminating evidence against Veronica, it wasn't kidnapping, was it?

Veronica had information, most likely evidence, that Jay needed to fully accomplish his undercover operation. If Toni was correct about where they were going, Jay had to believe that said evidence was at the Clayton mansion.

Wil looked in the rearview mirror, hoping to catch Jay's glance. Not for anything more than professional reasons, of course. But his attention was locked on the road, and as he took one last turn, she saw why. A sprawling estate loomed from the acres and acres of trees that kept it otherwise hidden. It looked like it belonged in the Alps instead of eastern Washington. Turrets rose from a stately building that boasted a brick facade, a parklike lawn complete with sculptured shrubs. Wil squinted to verify what she thought she'd seen at first glance. Yes, no question. One bush was pruned to look like a beaver, the shrub adjacent to it shaped like a fallen log. For all their money, the Claytons lacked the class that Veronica had so desperately tried to buy since she'd married Cal.

The entrance gate was a wrought iron monstrosity, complete with a very official-looking guardhouse.

"Cover her hands with these." Jay tossed his jacket and a backpack between the SUV's front seats. "Veronica, you're going to give zero indication that you're here for any other reason than to visit your husband."

"Never." She sneered. "Why the hell should I listen to you?"

"Because I'm a federal agent whose sole purpose for the last two years has been to bring Badger down. You'll never acquire the Mexican cartel," he said.

"Sure you are. You're working for Hector, I know it!" She growled the name of the Mexican cartel kingpin, whom Wil had read about. "You're no more a fed than this one was in the military!" She shot Wil a disparaging glance.

You are so wrong.

"There's enough evidence on you and your entire syndicate to put you all away for life. Your only hope for a more comfortable lockup is if you cooperate. I can't promise, but if you do as I say, it might encourage me to recommend that a judge sentence you to a federal corrections facility for life instead of what you deserve. Capital punishment is still in effect for certain federal crimes which you have committed. Do I need to make your options any clearer?"

Veronica's expression didn't change, not a difficult accomplishment considering the obvious Botox and fillers that her face sported, but her shoulders sagged and she let out a long sigh.

"Fine."

Jay seemed confident, in full-on law enforcement mode. It was encouraging, but Wil knew that any op could go south at any minute. She held her breath as they pulled up to the gate and a hulk of a man peered into the back seat. Veronica explained they were all coming in "to have an executive meeting with Cal."

The guard's eyes narrowed, fixated first on Jay, then lingered on Wil. She offered her best noncommittal glare. After an excruciating three heartbeats, he nodded.

"Okay, then, Mrs. Clayton. Let me know if you need anything more." He went back into the elaborate brick gatehouse that was a far cry from the guard shacks where Wil had stood countless watch rotations in the Marine Corps.

Jay drove slowly through the opened gates, entering the circular drive. They pulled up to the front double-door entrance and he killed the engine. She kept the keys in her jacket's inside pocket, since the vehicle was a keyless start.

If she thought the estate was impressive from the road, getting closer only reinforced her observation. Wil knew that logging could be a lucrative business, but the Mack website and staff size gave no indication of being able to afford its owner this level of luxury. If she hadn't believed that the Claytons were holding the reins on a large criminal syndicate before now, this alone would have convinced her.

"What do you expect to get from me here?" Veronica hissed. "Do you think I keep all the secret codes in my home?" She tried to make air quotations around *secret codes* but could only lift her cuffed hands so far. Frustration was mirrored in her snarl. "You're in way over your head here, Jay. Or whatever your damn name is."

Jay ignored her and met Wil's gaze in the rearview mirror. "Untie her feet and arms."

"Roger that." Wil thought he was nuts but also knew she'd have no problem restraining Veronica again if she had to.

"Make any move other than what I tell you and Wil is

going to stop you. Just as with the security guard, you're going to tell your house guard that you're here to see Cal. The same with his caretaker."

When Veronica didn't reply, Jay pressed. "Remember, you have a choice as to where you're going to spend the rest of your life."

"Got it." Veronica's chin rose, but her bottom lip was trembling. It was the first sign of vulnerability from the woman other than her weaker physical nature that Wil had witnessed. She used her Swiss knife's scissors to clip the plastic zip ties, careful to be ready to subdue Veronica.

"Here." Jay thrust a cell phone at Wil. "Enter her security code."

Wil held the phone in front of the woman's face, unlocking it, then entered the numbers Veronica told her.

"Gary won't open the door until I step on the porch steps." Veronica's resigned tone as she mentioned her in-home security agent indicated she was accepting her fate. Wil wasn't buying it. If she were in Veronica's place, she'd play along until the first opportunity to outsmart them.

Or kill you.

True to Veronica's description, the front door opened and a short, portly man stood on the threshold as they made their way up the steps. Steps that, if Wil's guess was right, were marble. Or at least granite. Judging from the rest of the house's outer decor, and the deep pockets the entire place required, it wouldn't have been beyond the Claytons' resources to import marble from Carrara, Italy, for their front entryway.

"You okay, Mrs. Clayton?" Gary asked. His bored expression revealed nothing.

"Of course I am. I'm so sorry I didn't phone ahead, but

there were a few complications at the office. These are business acquaintances of Cal's."

Gary ignored Jay and Wil. Clearly he left the security considerations to the gate guard. "No problem, Mrs. Clayton."

"We'll make our own way. Thank you, Gary."

Veronica led them to the front stairs, which were sweeping and steep. As they proceeded up the steps with Veronica in front and Wil and Jay to the rear, Wil thought there had to be an elevator somewhere that Cal Clayton used. Her elderly grandparents were still spry, but they wouldn't be able to climb these stairs without lots of rest along the way.

At the top of the landing, Veronica turned right down a long wing; it was too wide and lengthy to be referred to as a hallway or corridor. Once out of sight of Gary, Jay went slightly to the front while Wil hung back, a more offensive posture to better keep Veronica in line. She ignored them, walking until she paused in front of the last door that occupied the full center of the wing.

Wil's attention had been on Veronica the entire time, but it didn't prevent her from glancing at the gallery of framed photographs on both the walls and several credenzas. There were more than one of two young girls. Were they of Veronica and her sister who disappeared? It was hard to imagine the callous, power-hungry Veronica Clayton as a happy-go-lucky young girl.

Veronica turned to face them both before she opened the doors.

"Now, listen to me for once. Cal isn't up to seeing visitors, and it's going against medical protocol—"

"Save it for the judge and jury." Jay cut her off. "Let us in. Now."

Her attempt at a caring countenance evaporated and her

ruthless gaze told Wil that if Veronica had a weapon in her hands, she'd use it on both her and Jay without compunction.

"You will both regret this." She turned to Wil. "I should have sent you packing from day one. I requested a male bodyguard, one with experience."

"Trust me, I have all the experience I need." Wil was done taking anything off this sad excuse of a human being. "Listen to what he's telling you."

"Do you really think he's going to even remember your name?" Her accusation cut through Wil's righteousness, right to her heart. "Don't imagine for one second that I didn't see that hickey on your neck. Let me guess, in real life you're a prostitute?"

Anger rushed heat to her face.

"Enough, Veronica. Open the door." Jay cut through the harsher words she'd been ready to unleash on the criminal.

Had she allowed her sense of loyalty toward Jay, her damn emotions, to affect her decision to assist him with this op? Did Cascade Confidential really need any intel she'd retrieve once the FBI took down Badger?

Too late.

They entered the spacious bedroom one by one, Veronica in front. Once Jay's gaze had swept over the space, he nodded at Wil and motioned with his hand that they'd each stand beside Mack's substitute CEO.

The real CEO lay in a hospital bed, his elderly form eerily still, save for the sheet's movement from his breathing. The man's cheeks were sunken, his eyes closed.

Wil had seen Marines in bad shape, had once given first aid to a Marine who'd been grazed by a bullet in a combat zone. But she'd never seen someone so apparently close to death yet still alive.

Wil swallowed. This was the violent man who'd built both a logging business and criminal syndicate from the ground up over the last fifty years. As difficult as it was to reconcile the figure in the hospital bed with such evil acts, let alone the photos of a younger man that hung in the Mack front lobby, it was the truth.

"Hi, sweetheart. Don't you try to get up, I'm here now." Veronica stood at the side of the bed as she spoke in a saccharine tone, but it didn't stop her from throwing another ugly glance at Wil and Jay. Her false outrage would be comic, something Wil would be hard-pressed to not laugh at if not for their circumstance.

"What are we looking for? What do you need from him?" She whispered into Jay's ear, behind Veronica's back. They stood at least fifteen feet from the bed, in the middle of the humongous room.

Jay didn't respond, except to step closer to the bed.

"What can upsetting him on his deathbed give you, you animals?" Veronica hissed, still standing next to Clayton, her hand on the thin blanket covering his frame. Wil found this sadder than the fact that Veronica had stolen the Clayton legacy from both Cal and his sons, even though it was a mostly dishonorable legacy. The woman wasn't even holding her dying husband's hand. Wil had never experienced anything like this, where evil was masked so cleverly and naturally. *A matter of course to these folks.*

Once again, doubt assailed her, made her stomach gurgle with anxiety. What kind of situation had she gotten herself into by staying with Jay to finish this out? Should she have listened to Toni—and Jay—and left before it was too late?

It's been too late ever since you made love to him.

Yeah, there was that. She put her hand on her holstered weapon. Just in case.

* * *

Jay stepped closer, emboldened by Veronica's hesitation as she stood next to Cal's deathbed. The man looked about to expire at any moment. Jay would call in EMTs as soon as he was assured Cal Clayton wouldn't be killed by Veronica, or by one of her security goons. He was also re-assured by Willow's presence behind and to his right. She stood between the closed door they'd entered and the hospital bed, her weapon drawn. No one was coming through that door without Willow taking them out.

"We don't have to bother him if you'll give me what you know I want, Veronica. I've already got your financials, down to the last pennies you've transferred to the syndicate outside Guadalajara, as part of your pretense to join forces with them. Are they the army of thugs you think will help your takeover? Because let me assure you, they will run for the hills the minute they know your entire power base has been compromised."

"I've no idea what you're talking about. There's nothing to compromise. And how dare you speak to me like this in front of my dying husband!" She was pouring on the drama, but Jay knew fear when he saw it. He'd caught her unaware by showing exactly how much he knew.

"Drop the pretense, Veronica."

"Who the hell are you? You're working for Guadalajara, aren't you? It's the only way you survived that hit—" Desperation tinged her words, making them sound more like a plea. He had her where he needed her: without a weapon or one of her minions like Derek to complicate his mission.

"You ordered the hit on me?"

"I didn't. Derek did. He was convinced you were a narc."

It was time to go all in.

"I told you. I'm FBI Special Agent Jayden Lambert. Your

entire operation has been compromised. We have evidence that you have taken the multilevel logging corporation your husband ran, with a side of fraud and tax evasion, to another level of criminality. You've already taken over several smaller, local crime rings and even the main threat out of Vancouver. You've been trafficking everything from drugs to underage persons, just like Cal did, but you've expanded your syndicate tenfold."

Veronica's arm fell from her husband's bed and her shoulders sagged. "If you already know all of this, why haven't you arrested me yet?"

"You know why. You know what we want." Jay wasn't going to spell it out for her. In his experience, at this point in a confrontation, the bad guy usually saw the writing on the wall and caved. Veronica was different in that he suspected underneath all the trappings money afforded her, something besides greed drove her.

"You want the names of the other players I've joined forces with, then." She deliberately avoided mentioning the Mexican cartel. No surprise there.

"Names and holdings, yes. And their account information," he said.

"I want a lawyer." Strong words, but the venom had receded. For now.

"Once you have a lawyer, there's nothing I'm going to do for you unless you've given me what I want." Jay had no intention of breaking the law, but Veronica didn't know that.

A soft gasp, obviously Willow's, reached his ears. Apparently she didn't know he was bluffing, either.

He risked a glance at her, to reassure her. But her weapon was no longer trained on the door, but at Veronica.

"Drop it or I'll fire." Her tone was nothing he was prepared for. She'd issued the ultimatum with deadly calm.

When he looked back at Veronica he understood. Willow wasn't aiming her handgun at Veronica, but at Cal Clayton.

The man near death held a .45 in his scrawny but very much alive hand. He swung it between Veronica and Willow, Jay included in the deadly arc.

"Get on the ground, facedown, hands and legs spread wide. All three of you!"

"Cal, oh my gosh, you're better! Honey, this is such a surpri—" Veronica attempted.

"I'll bet it is. Get down before I blow your two-timing head off. Did you think you'd get away with drugging me? Nurses can be paid off, too, you know." The entire time Cal spoke, he didn't take his gaze off Jay and Willow.

Something deep inside Jay's chest exploded in a ball of heat. His mission, the objectives of the FBI, nothing mattered as much as one of the women Cal was aiming at. Willow.

No way would he let this SOB hurt her.

"I'll bet you weren't expecting this, were you, Mr. G-man? Did you all really think I wasn't onto my wife's evil doings?" He kept his gaze on them as he climbed from the bed, clad in a rumpled pajama top, blue jeans and cowboy boots. How long had Cal Clayton played the dying husband?

"I said it once already." He pointed at Willow. "Drop your weapon, honey, or I'll shoot this handsome man in his tracks." Cal turned back to Jay. "Don't even think of pulling your weapon, Mr. G-man, or I'll shoot first. I warn you, I'm a crack shot. But I assume you already know that, don't you?"

Jay did know that. Even taking into consideration Cal Clayton's age and recent illness—which he now doubted—

the man was capable of killing all three of them before anyone else got a shot off.

Save Willow.

"Drop your weapon, Wil." Jay spoke quietly, stalling for time, not wanting to rattle the elder Clayton. The man had feigned near death, perhaps even this illness, for long enough to have figured out what his wife was up to. Long enough to plan his own escape, with a side of ultimate revenge.

"I'm putting my pistol on the table next to the bed." Willow took several steps toward Cal Clayton and the very weapon that he could fire at any moment. Jay's breath stopped as his heart banged deep inside his chest. "There you go." She placed her weapon on top of a table covered with medical supplies and backed away.

"I said down on the ground! Veronica's not stupid, she's listening. Aren't you?" Cal walked from the side of his bed to stand at its foot, but not before he stomped loudly onto Veronica's hands and sent the gruesome sound of crunching bones through the air. Veronica's tortured scream told Jay all he needed to know. The man had broken several of his wife's fingers, if not her hands.

"Let my bodyguard go, Clayton. She's an innocent bystander in this." He made a motion with his right hand for Willow to keep standing.

Don't get on the ground. If only Wil could read his mind.

"I'm calling the shots, not you!" To emphasize his point, he fired into the air at the ceiling. Plaster rained down over the bed. "Go on, then, get out of here. And don't even think about sticking around to save this idiot." His barrel lowered, aimed at Jay's heart. "My sons are aware of what that lying bitch did to me. As is my nurse, who happens to be my son's fiancée. How do you think I've fooled her that I was still drugged to the gills?" He cackled long and hard as his wife emitted pained whimpers from the floor. The man was unhinged at best.

Jay gave Willow what might be his last glance at anyone. If he expected her eyes to reflect despair or concern, though, he'd have been a fool. Her steadfast gaze conveyed confidence, and something else he did not want to identify. Not now.

Had she figured a way out of this, against all odds?

"Go, Wil." It came out harsher than he'd have wanted, but no matter how much training, how many hours he'd rehearsed scenarios exactly like this one, nothing had prepared him to face his worst fear.

Wil didn't respond except to back out of the room, into the hallway.

"And shut the door behind your ass, girly." Cal was definitely used to being the boss.

Once the *click* of the door closing confirmed Wil was safe, Jay stared at the man responsible for at least sixteen deaths over the last decade, most by proxy but one or two by his own hands.

Was he the next one to be added to Cal Clayton's body count?

Wil closed the bedroom door but made sure she hadn't locked it, that the hinge doorknob still had full movement. She was on autopilot, leaning on years of Marine training. She pulled the pistol she'd stowed in an ankle holster out, held it in front of her and began to clear the corridor. She peered over the elaborate balcony into the grand foyer. No "butler," no other thugs on their way up the stairs to rescue Cal Clayton.

The man was wily, she'd give him that. And he had to

have had the cooperation of his nurse to get off the drugs the FBI had told Jay he was being kept prisoner with. No one was in this wing, from her quick scan. It appeared word had gotten out that the Clayton cartel was under threat. Instead of protecting Cal, though, his security hounds had split.

She knew she couldn't reenter the room through the doors she'd exited. But the French doors on the other side of Cal's bed, the picturesque view of the rolling mountains, told her she had another entry point. Time wasn't on her side. She ran for the stairs.

Wil turned to descend the steps, but her hip bumped against a decorative table, shaking a collection of framed photographs and knocking several down. She stopped in her tracks and held her breath. Had anyone heard her? Was there anyone still around to hear? Her training forced her to remain planted where she was for longer than her nerves wanted, but precaution necessitated. As she stood there, her gaze was drawn to the photos.

They were all photos of girls, and it was pretty obvious that the center girl in each of the photos was Veronica, whose basic facial features hadn't changed much save for her cosmetic injectables and over-the-top makeup. But the other girl—

Wil's stomach flipped. It was one of the girls who'd disappeared on the mining corporation's land. Another photo was the same one that had been used by law enforcement when the young girls had disappeared from Pine Hills thirty-five years ago. She did the quick math. The girls who disappeared had been ten. Veronica would have been six years old. So it was her older sister who was one of the missing girls.

"I said get down!" Cal's roar was dim but his tone unmistakable from the end of the wing, where she'd left the door cracked. Her cold case would wait.

Continuing to clear the spaces as she went, Willow ran down the stairs, through to the back of the house, to the kitchen. Not a single soul appeared or sounded. It wasn't what she'd expect but she wasn't questioning it. Not when Jay's life depended on her speed.

The kitchen was a French Provincial nightmare of distressed white oak and gold fixtures. She cut through a butler's pantry—this one stocked with high-tech gear from routers to security cameras—and into a large entryway she supposed was some kind of mudroom. Or would be a mudroom, in a normal residence.

The Clayton fortress, like the family, was nothing close to normal. She opened the outside door and carefully scanned the side of the house. A brick path led to the back area, where she hoped she'd find a way to climb up to Cal's balcony.

Go, go, go.

She had to reach Jay. Before one of Cal's bullets did.

Chapter 30

You lie down, you die.

Jay had been in several tight spots during his FBI career, but never one as seemingly impossible as this one. His team would have called in SWAT by now, he was certain. This far out in the mountains, the speed of their arrival—not to mention the time it would take them to neutralize any remaining Clayton goons—made the odds of them saving him negligible. Was this how his career, his life ended? Facing down an elderly albeit spry nonagenarian whose estranged arm-candy wife, equally manipulative and with the same power-hungry goals, lay on the floor? They might hate one another, but they hated federal law enforcement all the more.

Cal glared at him.

"I said get down! Last chance!" Cal's sure motion with the handgun, sweeping from between Jay's eyes to the floor and back, conveyed the expectation of a man used to having his every word obeyed. Taken as gospel. Except—Cal had suffered. He'd fallen victim to Veronica's evil machinations, until he was saved—by whom? His sons? Jay racked his memory, recalling each man's agency profile. The eldest, Fred, was ensconced in Cancun, managing the drug trafficking in and out of the Yucatan. Toby Clayton had left the US for either the Caribbean or South America; the intel reports indicated he'd used a fake passport to exit the country under a pseudonym and then had fallen off the grid.

Who had gotten Cal off the drugs that held him hostage the past two months? Were they about to emerge from behind him, put a bullet in his back?

Dig deep and stay the course. He had to use every last ounce of his negotiation training.

He held his hands up. "We both know I'm not going to do that, Cal. I'll tell you what I told Veronica. You can get a decent plea deal if you surrender now. That starts with taking your aim off a federal agent. It's not worth it, Cal." As he spoke, Veronica used her elbows to get to her feet, tottering once she stood.

"Don't listen to him, bab—"

"Shut up!" Cal's left arm slammed against Veronica's chest, knocking her back several feet. To her credit, she remained standing despite the ridiculously high-heeled shoes she still wore and the tremendous pain her broken hands must be causing. "I'll deal with you later. Sit on the bed. Now!" he barked.

To Jay's amazement, Cal managed to keep his weapon pointed at him the entire time. But at least he hadn't told him to lie down again. His eyes glittered with loathing as he refocused on Jay.

"I kept my side of the street clean, G-man. There's nothing on me that will put me behind bars. You'll get nothing from me or anyone else, either. I've been accused of a lot of things in my long life, but being a snitch is one I've never earned. You forget who you're dealing with."

"Veronica has sealed your fate. She's left a trail of evidence exposing your operations over the last two years. We know you joined forces with Badger, and you're about to partner with the Mexican cartel." He avoided using *take-over*. Let Clayton think he didn't know everything.

"I never agreed to any of that!" he growled, casting a scathing look at his wife. "You've ruined us. It was never enough to enjoy my riches, was it? Nothing is ever good enough for you. You forget where you come from—you're a nobody!"

"You should have known I wasn't in it for your pecker, Cal." Veronica's retort was surprising considering her present situation with her husband, but Jay welcomed her sparring with Cal. Because in the moment of her distracting him, Jay's peripheral vision caught movement beyond the large French doors.

SWAT.

Thank goodness. He only had to keep Cal talking, and if Veronica would distract him...

He looked again at the balcony. Nothing. Had he imagined it? Where the hell was SWAT? He'd sent a request to his team before he and Willow had left Mack, told headquarters he had Veronica with him.

"What are you looking at, G-man?" Cal sneered. Jay thought he'd been covert, but a man like Cal Clayton hadn't gotten as far as he had in such a cutthroat line of business without having extraordinary perception. Even at ninety-plus years. Of course he'd noticed Jay's torn attention.

Jay leaned into his mistake, held his breath. He turned his head and looked at the French doors that led to the balcony. This time his peripheral vision didn't let him down as he saw Cal turn to see where Jay's focus had been. The split second was all Jay needed.

He lunged for Cal.

Wil's phone vibrated against her thigh for the sixth time in two full minutes. Precious moments that might be Jay's last on earth.

Do. Not. Go. There.

Cal had been foolish to not have Veronica pat Wil and Jay down. She'd kept three pistols and her phone, no problem. Her settings allowed for vibration notification from Toni only. Toni would have to wait…

The phone shook again.

"Damn it!" she whispered to herself as she ducked behind one of the grotesquely shaped boxwood shrubs. Wil pressed the answer button on her earpiece.

"I can't talk, I'm in the middle of saving Jay from Cal Clayton!" She kept scanning the landscape as she spoke, her senses hyperalert.

"You can't go in there. SWAT is still fifteen minutes out." Toni's clipped tone mirrored Wil's tension. "Stay down and stay out, Willow."

"SWAT?" She paused. "Of course. That makes sense. Jay must have alerted his team. Fifteen minutes is too long. I can't wait, Toni. Cal's going to kill Jay. And probably Veronica, too."

"Wait—you have Veronica?" Surprise bloomed in Toni's voice. "Derek told the FBI she'd taken off," Toni continued. "Derek was apprehended as he tried to leave Mack, loaded for bear with weapons Veronica, and previously Cal, kept stored in the secret room."

"Wow. I'm glad they stopped him. I can't explain everything right now, but here's what you need to know and can pass to LE." She gave Toni the bare bullet points. "Turns out Cal was on to Veronica's game and faked being drugged until today."

"Which means he knew you and Jay, or at least Jay, were more than you let on. FBI just identified a local police officer who's been privy to the FBI undercover op for logistical reasons. Turns out he's an informant for Fred Clayton."

"Fred?"

"He's one of two sons who help run the crime syndicate. The other one is in South America somewhere, runs things from afar. Listen to me, Willow." Wil rolled her eyes. *Here it comes.* "We don't have eyes on Fred, Cal is holding Jay hostage, and help is too far away for you to go barging in there. I'm telling you to cease ops, Willow. It's not an ask."

Willow made a crunching noise. "Wha…can't…break-ing…"

"Willow O'Malley, do *not*—"

Wil hit her earpiece button and continued toward the back of the house, ignoring the immediate, subsequent calls from Toni.

Sorry, sis. Forgive me.

Toni would forgive her, once this was over. She was family and understood more than anyone that Wil would die for her family. Without realizing it until this very moment, one other person had joined Wil's definition of family over these last days.

Wil would do whatever it took to save Jay's life.

Wil was so close, yet too far to make a difference. Not as long as she was on the other side of the doors. She was flattened against the wall of the house, weapon drawn and ready to fire. But she'd have to fire through the glass, pray that she hit Cal Clayton before he could get a shot off. And then there was Veronica, who'd know where there was an extra weapon in the room. There had to be more weapons around. The Claytons were hardened criminals with a lot to protect.

Jay was there without a weapon. It seared through her, the thought of him taking a shot, of, of…

No.

It was then that she heard the scream.

* * *

"Cal, look out!" Veronica's scream all but pierced Jay's eardrums as his shoulder landed in the elder Clayton's gut.

"Oof." The air swished from Cal's lungs and the man crumpled beneath Jay, saliva flinging everywhere as he gasped, his mouth making crazy motions as though he were a fish flailing on dry land.

Jay was astride Clayton, reaching for the old man's pistol. He pulled up short when he spied Cal's empty hand. He must have dropped the—

Cold steel pressed into his temple.

"Get up, you stinking coward." Veronica let several more unsavory adjectives fly as she pressed the gun painfully against his skull. It had to hurt her hand. But not enough to keep her from being able to fire the weapon.

Jay had never felt so stupid. He could take out Veronica with one quick grab of her wrist and a duck, twist the weapon from her hand. But it risked her firing the gun, in turn risking either her or Clayton's death. Jay had worked too long, his team had toiled through too many wee hours as they'd tracked these two megalomaniacs. They were going to face their justice in a court of law if he had anything to do with it.

So he opted for negotiation.

"Don't do anything stupid, Veronica. The FBI already knows what you've done. Don't compound it with murder in the first of a government agent."

"Don't listen to him, Veronica." Cal was still on his back, his eyes staring straight ahead and his hands on his stomach. His words sounded as if he had a mouth full of marbles. Jay risked a look at him and realized it wasn't marbles but a bloody foam at his mouth that slurred the man's speech.

"Don't you worry, sugar. I've got him right where we

need him." Veronica motioned at Jay with the gun. "Get him up and on the bed. Then you and I are going to have a little chat."

Jay carefully got to his knees, then lifted the ailing man. Cal Clayton continued his labored breathing as Jay moved him back to the bed. The man was heavier than he would have expected for one so frail. Maybe evil deeds weighed a body down over a lifetime.

Once Clayton was back atop the hospital mattress, Jay turned to Veronica. She nodded with satisfaction.

"There, that wasn't so hard, was it? Keep your hands up! Now, let's figure out what it is that you want, Mr. FBI man."

"What I want is for you to put that gun down before you make this worse than it already is. It's over, Veronica. SWAT has surrounded this place. There are at least three sharpshooters with your head in their sights." He prayed his words were true. Or that she'd believe them, true or not.

He should be thinking about how to get out of this alive, with both suspects also intact. He'd probably given Cal a lethal blow and Veronica was pointing a gun at his head. Yet all he could do was wonder if Wil had made it to safety.

And pray he'd live to see her again.

Chapter 31

Wil risked looking into the bedroom from the balcony. Jay was placing Cal Clayton onto the hospital bed. She couldn't see the elderly man's face, but she saw Veronica.

Pointing Cal's revolver at Jay's head, with the hand that must have been least injured. Veronica was yelling, waving the gun around as if it were a toy, and Jay started to slowly turn around, his hands raised.

Wil tried the balcony door handle. To her relief, it quietly clicked open. If she'd had to kick it down, the noise would have given Veronica too much warning. Wil was quick, as was Jay, but it was impossible to outmaneuver a bullet once it left the barrel. Slowly, slowly she inched through the doors, until she could stand behind the floor-length drapes. From there she moved the fabric back the few inches she needed to have a clear view of the scene.

"You're crazy to think I'm ever going to give you the evidence you want, Jay. And without it, you don't have a case." Veronica's voice didn't resemble the cool cucumber she'd portrayed at Mack. She sounded decidedly confused, threatened.

"Look at the facts, Veronica. With a good legal team, you can get out of this with at most several years in a cush situation, compared to what you'll get if you kill a federal officer. You have a lot of information that's valuable to the government. Use it to your best interest." Jay spoke as easily as he did in the car when they were having a meal or coffee together. Not like a man whose life was a small finger pull from extinction.

No. He's not going to die.

"Don't try to manipulate me!" Veronica shrieked. "I'll never give you what you want!" She took one step back and looked over her shoulder. Wil quickly leaned back and held her breath behind the heavy drapes. Had she been seen?

Click, click. Veronica drew closer, closer. Was the woman going to shoot Jay and then exit via the balcony? Was Jay forcing her to walk backward?

Wil wasn't going to wait to find out. She knelt down, and when Veronica was dead even with her, she grabbed the woman's ankle and tugged.

"No!" Veronica's scream punctuated the sight of her body flying through the air, her arms spread wide. She slammed down onto the balcony's tiled deck, body first and then her head. The crack of her skull sounded a split second before her eyes closed. The gun remained in her hand. Wil moved to take the weapon, but strong, familiar hands reached it first.

"Thank you."

She looked up into Jay's gaze. "Wait." She looked at Veronica, who remained still.

She placed her fingers on the woman's jugular. A strong pulse knocked against her fingertips. "She's alive. You'll have your day in court."

Jay stood, shoved Veronica's weapon in his back waistband. Wil mirrored him, but not intentionally. His gaze locked with hers, and they stepped away from Veronica's inert form. His hand was hot as he grasped her upper arm and pulled her back into the bedroom, putting a thick wall of security between them and any possible threat that lurked outside.

She took in Cal's still body on the hospital bed. "Is he—"

"No more talking." His hands were on either side of her face, his thumb lifting her chin as she jumped up against him, locking her legs behind his waist. Their mouths met in a union of relief and celebration, yes. But so much more. Jay's tongue claimed hers, tasting of pure Jay. She gave as good as she got from him, trying to pour in every single emotion he'd sparked alive in her since the first time their eyes met in the diner.

Sirens sounded simultaneously with the chopping sound of helicopter blades. Wil didn't care, didn't ever want this moment to end. Because when it did, the outcome was not something she wanted to ever face.

A life without Jay.

Chapter 32

Jay made himself a third cup of espresso inside the van just as dawn broke. Taking the stainless steel mini mug with him, he took it outside and sat in the camping chair Willow had left behind. He was torturing himself, but it couldn't be helped. Sitting in the armed rocker—thanks to two small hydraulic pumps, one on each side of the chair—was as close as he'd ever get to being in Willow's arms again.

What a sap he was.

"I'll be in touch." His last words to her weren't what haunted him as much as the warmth, the damned hope in her hazel depths. He knew better than to ever tell a woman he'd be in touch. But with Willow, he could. For the sake of the legal case. She'd definitely be called to testify if the Claytons didn't plead guilty on all charges.

You need to call her.

He took a sip of the bold brew and let his gaze wander over the clear aquamarine of Flathead Lake, Montana. He'd had to get out of Washington and blamed his need to cleanse his mind of the case and his undercover persona. Who was he kidding? The unexpected relationship with Willow had driven him away, as emotional intimacy had never been his forte. He was protecting her from the inevitable—his inability to commit. Wasn't he?

Nearby trees shed their leaves in a rainbow of autumnal hues, the gold ones reminding him of the flecks in Willow's eyes. If she was with him, he could spread a blanket out here, serve her fresh eggs with the espresso. Make love to her with the distant snowcapped mountains their only witness.

There's your problem. Love. Yeah. he'd never thought of anything but having sex with Willow before they had, and ever since, he couldn't think of the passion they'd shared as anything *but* lovemaking.

"What's a lifelong single dude to do?" He asked the rhetorical question to a squirrel that had leaped across the pebbled shore with a huge chestnut in his mouth. The squirrel froze at his voice, but didn't deign to solve his existential angst about the opposite sex.

It wasn't about just any member of the opposite sex, though. This was all about Willow.

His leave didn't begin until midnight tonight. Not officially. But the op was over and Janice had encouraged him to "take off." They'd worked hard to wrap up the remnants of Badger and its attempts to take over the PNW. It'd been the three longest weeks of Jay's life. Not because of the long hours, entering all the data the courts would need to prosecute Cal and Veronica Clayton. Whatever it took to get the scum of the earth behind bars was no bother, as far as he was concerned. Nor did the middle-of-the-night wake-up calls from his overstressed mind concern him. It was always hard letting go of an op, but the fact was that once the bad guys were caught, the most he'd have to do with them ever again was to testify in a court of law. Period. It was the constant thrum of regret in his chest that bothered him.

Had he made a mistake by letting Willow go? Or was

this uncomfortable emotion, an anxious foreboding, because of the two Claytons who remained at large?

FBI headquarters had confirmed one Clayton son, Toby, was living in Buenos Aires, where he had presumably run cyberlogistics for Mack from there, utilizing the dark web as much as possible. When Mack shut down last week, Toby had disappeared, but the FBI was certain he remained in Argentina. For now.

Cal's other son, Fred, remained on the lam somewhere in North America, most likely in the Pacific Northwest, last spotted in British Columbia, Canada, which meant he'd traveled up from Mexico. Jay figured he had been ferreting out the dirt on a crime syndicate in Vancouver. But he'd disappeared from agency detection means within hours of the takedown at the Clayton estate.

Jay was relieved Cal was alive to hopefully receive a life sentence in prison, but time was working against him. Cal was a strong, stubborn son of a bitch. With a long history of violence, once on his feet and imprisoned, the criminal would be issuing commands from his cell by any means possible. Which of course it was, with his slick defense lawyer who specialized in getting the worst of the worst out of legal jeopardy. The Clayton attorney wasn't going to get Cal off this time, Jay was certain. But he'd make sure all of Cal's civil rights were provided, which meant Cal could talk to his sons regularly enough to cause havoc.

His phone vibrated. Janice. He hadn't heard from her since she'd confirmed the body of the motorcycle driver and shooter had been found, along with a very mangled bike. He'd been hired by Derek to 'threaten' Jay. Derek still claimed that he didn't hire the thug to assassinate Jay.

Janice was calling to make sure he was going to take his break, no doubt.

"Hi, Janice. I promise, I'm taking leave. I'm already in another state, as a matter of fact," he said.

"Where are you?" She sounded rushed, or excited. She hadn't called for small talk.

"Flathead Lake. Montana. Leaving here in an hour or two."

"Change that. You're heading out now. Hang on." She paused and he waited. Janice wasn't overly dramatic, but she always needed a few breaths to get her thoughts in order. "Listen. We had a solid hit on Fred Clayton's location three hours ago."

"Where?"

"Coeur d'Alene Lake, no more than a block from Willow's condo."

Cold fear turned the espresso he'd drank into battery acid in his gut. "Was, did—"

"No, no, she's fine, she wasn't there. But he was looking for her, is my guess. You know the Claytons as well as I do, Jay. Better than me. Revenge never escapes them."

"Tell me where the bastard is now." He'd take him out with his bare hands if need be. He threw the chair into the van, took down the sunshade, secured his coffee pot. Damn it! Willow did not deserve this.

Willow.

"We haven't had another hit on Fred, and I tried Willow's phone, but she's either not picking up, doesn't have it on her, or is ignoring unknown calls. The cell reception is spotty at best where she's headed, to boot."

"You think he has her?" His stomach twisted.

"No, but he's definitely tracking her. The entire O'Malley family is congregating in Montana at their parents' new place, near Seeley Lake. It's only a little over an hour from you. If you leave now, you can get there at the soonest Fred can. If that's indeed where he's heading."

"Got it." Fastening his seat belt, he started the van's engine.

"Hold on, Jay. Do not act on your own. He may have backup with him. I can't alert the local LE, as we're not sure if they're in cahoots with the Claytons, or were, with Badger. I need you to call in for reinforcement on your sat phone when you get there and assess the situation."

"Will do." Jay disconnected with only one thought pounding in his heart.

Save Willow.

Wil swiped tears from her cheeks as she drove to her parents' new home in Montana. Twenty-three days that felt more like twenty-three years since she'd seen Jay. Since he'd promised he'd "be in touch." It was her parents' big day, even if they didn't know it yet. All of the O'Malley siblings were descending upon their retirement nest in celebration of their anniversary.

Toni had wanted to drive together, but Wil begged off, using the excuse of needing time alone to process the facts she'd put together about the cold case. Toni accepted her reasoning, but Wil knew that her sister was worried about her. As evidenced by this, her third phone call in as many hours.

"How far out are you?" Toni asked. Wil looked at her phone, attached to her Jeep's dash with a rickety holder. It was the first long trip she and her beloved vehicle were enjoying, and while she missed the high tech of the Cascade Confidential armored SUV, she enjoyed riding in her Wrangler more.

"Another couple of hours. How about you two?" she asked. Toni's daughter was in the car with her.

"We're almost there," Toni replied.

"What are you going to say to them? Don't blow this surprise!"

"I won't. I told them that Sierra can't wait to see their place all finished, and they bought it."

"Aunt Willow, Mom's got all the frets over you right now. She doesn't believe me that you said you are happy living by yourself," twelve-year-old Sierra interjected. "Please tell her you're fine."

Wil grinned. "I'm perfectly fine, honey. And hey, heartache is part of life."

"This is why you don't need a man to make your life whole," Toni said. Wil rolled her eyes.

"Stop it! Men are great, Sierra. Relationships can be wonderful, too. But remember, love is an action—"

"I know, I know." Sierra's exasperation was right on target. Wil remembered being annoyed by anything her parents or aunts and uncles said to her about life at that age. "But I'm not like either of you."

"You're not?" Wil and Toni spoke in unison.

"No. I'm in touch with my emotions," Sierra said.

"Thanks for letting us know," Toni said. "Wil, without going into details, try to remember what I suggested earlier."

She'd asked her to reach out to Jay, let him know how she was feeling. Wil refused. Ripping off the bandage instead of allowing her heart to break piece by piece was preferable. She wasn't in the mood to repeat it, though, and not in front of her niece. Sierra deserved a more positive outlook on romance, at least for now.

"Gotcha. Look, I wasn't kidding about wanting time to think about the Hartford case. I'll talk to you when I get there."

Toni sighed. "Okay, see you soon."

"Bye, Aunt Willow!" Sierra chimed. "Mom, put my music back on."

Wil disconnected.

Toni had been excited about the headway she was making on the case. Wil was more cautious in her enthusiasm. Sure, she had made inroads, but it could take months longer to solve it. Once she'd verified Veronica as the blood sister of one of the missing girls, she'd gone straight to the source, who was in jail. Veronica had confessed that her motive and drive to become the most powerful kingpin in North America had begun after her big sister had disappeared. The case had never been solved, but locals believed a mining company had something to do with their fate and had had the funds to shut down the more thorough investigation the families of the victims called for. Veronica had spilled the beans when Wil visited her in the local county jail just days after the takedown. As much as she'd gotten out of Veronica, the deposed kingpin and former Mack CEO wouldn't say who she believed had taken the three. Nor would Veronica reveal if she believed they were all deceased, as most had presumed.

Except for the lone woman who'd shown up at Wil's Coeur d'Alene office, seeking closure on the case. Hoping against hope that her loved one was still alive, somewhere.

As of this morning, Veronica was being held in prison, without bail, awaiting trial. Cal Clayton was still in the hospital, conscious but on the edge of life. If he lived long enough, both he and Veronica would stand trial. Which was good for Jay; she was happy for him.

That's where her generosity for the man who'd changed her life but hadn't been interested in sticking around ended.

Keep telling yourself that.

Chapter 33

The mountain highway yielded to a high, flatter road as Wil continued her drive. The elevated plain allowed for a spectacular view of the valley below, where her parents had opted to spend their retirement. A smile tugged on her lips even while her heart was heavy with letting go of Jay. It would be good to see her brothers, her sisters, her niece all together. One thing about the O'Malleys—they knew how to laugh and enjoy a party.

Two hours after they'd last spoken, her phone rang and she answered, hands-free.

"Hi, Toni."

"Where are you? Even the boys are here. They're still hanging out half a mile away, waiting for you to show up so we can all say 'surprise' together." Toni laughed.

"I'm ten minutes out." She put on her turn blinker, noting a Ford F-250 pickup behind her slowing to do the same. "Anyone else coming besides the family?" As she spoke to her sister, a beep sounded, indicating another incoming call. She ignored it, keeping her focus on the road.

"So far I've met three different neighbors, but that's it."

"That sounds perfect!" She forced cheer into her reply.

"But you don't sound so good, sis. You're still hoping he'll reach out?" Toni sighed, conveying volumes.

"I know what you think, and you have good reason to." Wil had watched Toni raise her daughter while sharing custody with her niece's biological father. Toni never complained or put Sierra's father down, but Wil knew whatever relationship Toni and Brandon had once shared, it was nothing more than coparenting today.

"It's a hard truth to accept. That what meant so much to you didn't mean the same to them. Not enough to stay." Toni's voice was quiet, her tone compassionate.

"The thing is, Jay and I didn't have lots of time together, obviously. And you know me, Toni. I'm not one to mistake a great time in bed for happily-ever-after. My life's been anything but a fairy tale. But Jay is…was different." She blinked. Toni was right. This hurt like hell.

"Maybe he'll get back to you eventually. But you can't put your life on hold until then. Now, get over here and let's have some fun! Wait until you see this place!" Toni's words were static filled, as the connection up here was catch-as-catch-can.

"Gotcha. Be there in a few."

Instead of continuing her drive to the house, though, she made a quick U-turn and went back to the grocery store she'd passed. So caught up in her own thoughts, she'd neglected to get flowers or treats for her parents and family. The siblings had all chipped in on one big anniversary gift, but she'd like to bring her mom flowers.

As she walked through the upscale market, she found high-end chocolates, a premade charcuterie board, champagne and a bouquet of the largest sunflowers she'd ever seen outside of a farm field. The caterers would be providing food and drink for the actual party, but she wanted to make sure there was enough for tomorrow, too, as everyone was staying at least two nights.

As she ran her items through the self-checkout, she vowed to put her broken heart—that had no reason to be broken—on hold and to show her family how much she loved them. Her parents were celebrating their wedding anniversary and a housewarming, both hard-won and well deserved. They deserved her happiest self.

She carried her purchases out to her Jeep, enjoying the way the breeze made her yellow dress sway, along with her lighter steps. A frown tugged at her lips, though, when she spied another large pickup truck, this time parked too close to her passenger side. Was it the same truck she'd noted behind her as she turned into town?

She recalled the tag number, which, thanks to Montana law, was displayed on the front fender. Rounding her vehicle, she read the rear license plate of the pickup.

Her nape prickled. It was the license plate, the same Ford F-250 that made the U-turn with her. Yet it hadn't followed her into the parking lot, but passed her as she turned in. Now it was next to her Jeep. The windows were tinted, making it impossible for her to see inside.

You're being paranoid.

She was. So what if the same truck was parked next to hers? Did no one else ever needed to get groceries on a beautiful Saturday morning?

Wil scanned the parking lot, the grocery store entry and the adjacent Chinese restaurant. Several families with young children in tow, a steady stream of mostly four-wheel-drive vehicles—in the mountains she'd expect nothing different—and two teenagers collecting errant carts and hauling them back to the store.

Nothing to see here.

"I'm going for a walk." Wil announced her intention to the crowded room, but no one replied. She and her brothers had met up on the main road just before her parents' driveway, and Toni had made her parents open the front door, at which point they all yelled, "Surprise!" In the hour since, lunch was served, drinks were poured and much laughter ensued.

Willow's heart still ached, but she refused to taint the festivities with her sadness, so she opted to check out her parents' land. At least, the acre of grass in the back of the house, before woods and mountains claimed their remaining thirty acres.

She quickly traded her dress sandals for the sneakers in her Jeep, then set off to walk across the back lawn. Her goal was to check out the edge of the woods, maybe spot a deer or twelve.

The light breeze lifted her hair from her neck and she gulped in the fresh air, the cedar aroma soothing. She was thirty-eight years old. This wasn't her first heartbreak, nor the first time a lover had ghosted her. "This, too, shall pass." She muttered the phrase aloud, as if hearing the words would make them real.

Allowing herself to relax and stop with the constant pretense of being thrilled for her parents—she was, but the weight of her heart made all that laughter and smiling a bit much—Wil moved into the woods. There were no clear paths available and she wore simple athletic sneakers, so hiking any farther in wasn't an option. Instead, she leaned against the nearest tree, uncaring if it snagged her favorite yellow dress. The irregular bark was something she could count on, a constant in the forest. If only Ja—

Snap.

She whirled, expecting to see a deer, or, hopefully not, a bear. Instead, a stranger decked out in camouflage hunting gear stood no farther than three feet from her. Relief flushed across her high alert. "I thought you were a bear."

The hunter sneered and lifted his rifle, pointed the end of the barrel between her eyes.

"I'm worse than a grizzly, Willow O'Malley. I'm Fred Clayton, and you're about to pay for messing up my life."

Willow gasped as cold, dark dread pumped through her veins. But before her self-recrimination over having been so stupid, so unaware of her surroundings crept in, her training took over. Above all else, she had to disarm him, for the sake of her family, who partied, unaware, close enough for his bullets to reach them.

Engage the enemy. Strike up rapport.

"Fred. Let's talk first, shoot later."

He didn't move his sight from her. "Claytons aren't big on talk, Willow." His gaze moved, and when it focused on her body, leering, a distinct rage ignited in her gut. *Use your anger to achieve your objective.*

"I'm sure we can work this out, Fred. I had nothing to do with what happened to your family." *Keep stalling him.*

"Bullshit. I was all ready to take down Veronica, to get the family business back where it belongs. Into my and my brother's hands. But no. You had to play security guard with that fake accountant and mess things up." He kept the weapon on her. "You think I couldn't find out who you worked for? A rent-a-cop place." He must have seen the surprise on her face. She swallowed.

"You were the one I chased out of the woods the other night, weren't you?"

"You didn't chase me, sweetheart. I left. I tried to warn you both off before that. Maybe you recall the black Mustang that almost ran you off the road?" His words immediately placed the memory of driving with Jay next to her, as she'd outmaneuvered Fred. *You outsmarted him once. You can do it now.*

"And you were on the motorcycle, too?"

He snorted. "No bike for me. I'm a Ford man all the way."

Relief that she was still standing, that Fred was still talking, was overshadowed by the determination in his eyes, the steely soulless stare that left no doubt what she was to Fred Clayton at this point. An easy target. She could drop, roll—

Crack.

The sound created the split-second reprieve she'd been hoping for. Fred kept his rifle pointing toward her, but his gaze shifted to the right. She didn't bother to look, didn't care what creature had made the noise, even if it was a grizzly bear. One of Fred's bullets would kill her first. But not if she could help it.

Wil lunged forward, grabbed the rifle barrel with both hands and twisted. It didn't move. Fred was stronger and overpowered her, forced her to the ground and straddled her. Wil kept her grasp on the rifle, though, kept the barrel pointed away from her.

"If you wanted some fun before I shoot you dead, you should have said something." He wrenched the rifle from her grip, threw it aside and raised his fist.

"No!" She tried to twist away while bracing for the punch.

A punch that never came. Instead, Fred let out a loud grunt before he collapsed on top of her, a dead weight. He was on her no more than a second before something lifted him away.

Where was the rifle? She had to kill the bear. It had to be a bear. She was on all fours now, crawling toward the weapon, reaching for it—

"Willow, it's me." Strong hands on her shoulders, stopping her. "You're safe."

Maybe she was already dead. She slowly raised her head, an inch at a time. Familiar hiking boots. Camping cargo pants. Dark jacket. Generous mouth.

Bright blue eyes that beseeched her with the same hunger that had gnawed at her these past three weeks.

"Jay. You—you came back?"

"I've been trying to reach you for the past hour. So has Janice, my partner. Where's your phone?"

She recalled the beeps when she was talking to Toni. "In my car."

"I knew I could get here at the same time as the last hit we had on Fred, but it wasn't certain enough. Willow, I could have lost you." His eyes reflected concern, anger, maybe despair, and…dare she think the same emotion that had her heart on fire?

"Oh, Jay…but wait!" Belatedly, she remembered Fred Clayton and looked at his prone form. "Oh. You came here to catch him." She couldn't help drawing the moment out, she'd dreamt of it every day since Jay had walked away.

"No, not for him. For you. Always for you, Willow. I've been a stupid, stupid fool. Can you forgive me?"

"Only if you promise to spend the rest of your life making it up to me." She didn't break eye contact as she got to her feet, as Jay took her hands in his and helped her up.

"Are you okay, Willow? Any hit to your head?" he asked, picking dried leaves from her hair.

"I'm perfectly clear, Jay. How about you?" She reached up, tentatively touched the scar where she'd placed butterfly bandages not too long ago. "It's healed nicely."

Sirens sounded, and Willow looked past his shoulder to

the back lawn, to where her family, all bearing either hand-guns or rifles, ran toward her.

"The cavalry's coming," she said. But all she cared about was the man standing in front of her. "We've been here before, Jay. Criminal knocked out, SWAT on the way."

"We have." He nodded, his blue eyes on fire with something deeper than regret or determination. She knew the same emotion reflected back to him from her eyes. "Except it's different this time, Willow. This time, I'm not letting you go."

"Jay, I lo—"

"Willow, I lo—"

Their declarations were cut off as their lips met.

* * * * *